From Pasties to Pilchards

From Pasties to Pilchards

Recipes and Memories of Cornwall

Catherine Rothwell

To my friends Alison, Barbara and Jen.

Front cover picture: Some of the author's old regional recipes in manuscript form.

Back cover picture: Organic vegetables at a Cornish market.

First published 2009

The History Press
The Mill, Brimscombe Port
Stroud, Gloucestershire, GL5 2QG
www.thehistorypress.co.uk

British Library Cataloguing in Publication Data.
A catalogue record for this book is available from the British Library.

ISBN 978 0 7524 4908 1

Typesetting and origination by The History Press
Printed in Great Britain

Contents

Acknowledgements

I would like to thank Barbara Strachan, Susan Eaton, Salmon & Co., St Ives Fisheries, Friends of Truro Cathedral, *The Falmouth Packet*, Esther Hendy, Jane Spencely, Barbara Musgrave, Cornwall Tourist Board, St Agnes Bakery, The County Museum, Truro, S.J. Grocutt, Chris Ramsey, The National Trust, Ruth Johns, Killiow Country Park, Mrs M. Satterthwaite, Bob Timmins, and Col. L.W. Smith.

Introduction

Setting off many years ago from our home in faraway Lancashire, getting to Cornwall was always a journey of particular excitement. In those distant childhood days it was such a long journey and, with no motorway, it meant getting up very early – fifty years later that was still our chosen way.

Setting forth on a more than usual adventure, leaving miles of uncluttered road behind as we sped through early morning mist patches and eight counties to reach the West Country, saw a mingling of pleasure and anticipation that has not lessened with the years.

What joy therefore, when our daughter and family moved to Cornwall, one of our favourite places, where, in 1950, our honeymoon was spent. At last the chance to make it a second home.

We enjoyed a sense of history, almost tangible in places like Zennor and Polmassick. There was the glorious colour pageantry of incomparable gardens and, of course, the sea in all its moods. How the appetite is sharpened by boisterous winds whipping in from the Atlantic. The memories of my first shared Cornish pasty eaten at Tintagel and Cornish Splits at Land's End are unforgettable.

As we moved around the county we lost no opportunity to talk to all and sundry. There was never any sense of being an intruder, rather was there eagerness to help and encourage, which made the task of collecting recipes lighter and more enjoyable. From the manor house at Trerice to the workmen's hut at Pendennis Point, the same spontaneous spirit emerged. Nostalgic memories of grandparents' cooking were recalled by housewives, farmers, gardeners, licensees, caterers, boatmen, curators, fishermen, bakers, vintners, sailors and miners.

Cornwall exploits its fresh local products; fruit, vegetables, fish, cream, yeast and meat – but that is not to say that more exotic, continental dishes don't have their place and exist alongside the simple and traditional. Use is made of local ingredients such as oysters, crab, lobster and other fish. The county's climate is suitable for growing fruit such as figs, peaches and grapes out of doors.

Whilst I was discussing food, I noticed a similarity to my native Lancashire – Cornishman M.J. Phillimore's penchant for granny's succulent tripe and onions, and his mother's Heavy Cake, longingly described, which brought to my mind Sad Cake.

Midsummer's Day in 1988 was memorable when the beacon was lit at St Agnes to celebrate not only the solstice, but also 19 July, the quatercentenary of the Spanish Armada. We were searching for traditional cooking pots, particularly a pipkin. As we climbed up from the main street, through quiet alleys lined with pastel-washed cottages and tumbling valerian and fuchsia, we found the Wayside Pottery, who made us a pipkin. The pottery has been operating in a converted barn since 1930. Later we discovered New Mills potter, John Davidson, of the Co-operative Shop Guild of Ten, who also specialised in making pipkins.

This collection of old Cornish recipes was assembled in a roughly coastwise direction, so anyone undertaking the National Trust cliff-top walks may well be following the same route that we did. Bread, the staff of life, was much in my mind at Port Quin where local tradition maintains that the women and children left this deserted village after its fishermen, husbands and fathers, were lost in a storm at sea. It was sad to think of all those hearthstones, once warm and in continuous use, growing cold. But, uninhabited in the nineteenth century, it is now a hamlet come to life.

There is no finer food than that prepared lovingly from fresh local ingredients, and that hope is expressed in the recipes that follow.

Imperial/Metric Equivalents and Oven Temperatures

1oz	25g
2oz	50g
3oz	75g
4oz	110g
5oz	150g
6oz	175g
8oz	225g
10oz	280g
12oz	350g
1lb	450g
2lb	900g
3lb	1.35kg
¼ pint	150ml
½ pint	275ml
1 pint	570ml
2 pint	1.21 litre

	°C	°F	Gas Mark
Very Cool	110	225	¼
	120	250	½
Cool	140	275	1
	150	300	2
Moderate	160	325	3
	180	350	4
Moderately Hot	190	375	5
	200	400	6
Hot	220	425	7
	230	450	8
Very Hot	240	475	9

Many old recipes referring to gills followed the old fluid measures. The original meaning has been retained, thus:

1 gill	¼ pint (150ml)
1 cup of sugar	4oz (110g)
3 cups of flour	12oz (350g)

PLACES A–Z

ANTHONY

Anthony is one of the great Cornish houses owned by the National Trust. The village of Anthony was first known as Churchtown and was part of the Exeter Diocese.

Straddling county boundaries as it does, one cottager joked that he slept with his head in Cornwall and his feet in Devon.

Long before 1420 there was a wooden church and the first school was built in 1766 by the Carew family. It has a splendid motto, 'Manners Maketh man', and what started as a school to help 'twelve poor children to read and write' now educates over 100.

Village names such as Wacker, Blerick and Shevik are not far away and there is a popular darts team known as the 'Tea and Bun Club' who play at the Ring o' Bells Inn.

Cornish Yeast Buns

Ingredients

4oz (110g) butter
1lb (450g) flour
½ teaspoon salt
4oz (110g) currants
2oz (50g) sultanas
4oz (110g) sugar
1oz (25g) yeast
½ pint (275ml) of warm milk

Method

- Mix one teaspoon of the sugar with a little of the warm milk and mix in the yeast. Leave in a warm place.
- Sift flour and salt and mix together then rub in the butter and add the fruit and sugar.
- Make a well in the centre of the mixture and add the yeast.
- Sprinkle a little flour over the mixture and in five minutes the yeast will be seen to rise through the flour.
- Add the rest of the milk and mix into a dough.
- Leave to rise in a warm place until dough doubles in size, about ¾ hour.
- Divide the dough into buns.
- Place on a greased, floured baking sheet.
- Cover with a cloth and allow a further 20 minutes to rise.
- Bake in a moderate oven 160°C/gas mark 3.

Shoulder of Lamb with Wild Thyme

As with trout, wrapping lamb in a parcel with herbs subtly flavours it from the outside to the bone.

Ingredients *(Serves 4)*

1 half shoulder of lamb
2 cloves of garlic
Olive oil for greasing
Sea salt and freshly ground black pepper
16 sprigs wild thyme
¼ pint (150ml) dry white wine
¼ pint (150ml) stock

Method

- Heat oven to 180°C/gas mark 4.
- Cut garlic into thin slivers.
- Cut slits into the lamb and insert the slivers of garlic.
- Grease a large sheet of greaseproof paper with the oil. Season the paper well.
- Lay 8 sprigs of the thyme on the paper and place lamb on top. Cover the lamb with the remaining thyme sprigs and wrap in the oiled paper.
- Wrap the parcel again in an ungreased piece of greaseproof paper and place in a roasting tin.
- Roast for 2 hours.
- Unwrap parcel while it is still in the tin to retain the juices.
- Place lamb onto a carving dish, and if necessary skim the juices.
- Put the tin with juices on top of oven over a high heat and pour in the wine and stock. Bring to the boil and simmer for 1 minute.
- Carve lamb and serve sauce separately.

Apple and Celery Salad with a Honey and Lemon Dressing

This recipe was recommended for combating arthritis and rheumatism. Bean sprouts can be added to the recipe for variety.

Ingredients

1 head of celery, well washed
2 dessert apples
The juice of 1 lemon
2 teaspoons of clear honey
Sea salt and ground pepper to taste

Method

- Slice the celery and apples.
- Combine all the ingredients together and toss well.
- Make the dressing by whisking together the lemon juice and honey.

BODMIN

A Way with Grouse

An old favourite dish and one that would be much appreciated after striding over Bodmin Moor, wild and dramatic and stretching for miles. St Petroc, who founded three monasteries in Cornwall, lived a hermit's life on the moor.

Ingredients

4 grouse
1 teaspoon salt
1 cup boiling water
1 cup Cornish cream
4 slices bacon
1 cup hot milk
½ teaspoon pepper
butter

Method

- Wash and dry birds.
- Fix slices of bacon around the breast of each bird – game birds need this fat to prevent stringiness.
- Sprinkle with salt and pepper.
- In the deep pan turn the birds over in the heated butter.
- Add boiling water very gradually to avoid splashing of the hot fat. Carefully add the milk.
- Simmer for 2½ hours with the cooking pot well covered with liquid. Stir in cream towards the end of cooking and give them a further 20 minutes.
- Stir a teaspoon of butter into the grouse gravy and serve with green peas, new potatoes and cranberry jelly.

BOSCASTLE

Boscastle is a typical Cornish fishing village which handled limestone, china clay, minerals, bricks and coal. It abounds in smuggling stories. In 1843 the *Jessie Logan* ran aground here and its carved ship's figurehead can still be seen. Villagers could boast that they drank water from the river garden at Gunpoal, their supply.

This recipe is linked with the novelist Thomas Hardy who walked with Emma, his wife, from St Juliet to Boscastle and which inspired one of his best novels, *A Pair of Blue Eyes*.

For two centuries, travellers obtained rest and good food at the Wellington Inn. At the top of the old coaching road is its 'opposite number', the Napoleon Inn!

Lentil and Carrot Soup

Ingredients

7oz (200g) lentils
2 large onions
2 cans of chopped tomatoes
2 large carrots
1¼ pint (725mls) of stock

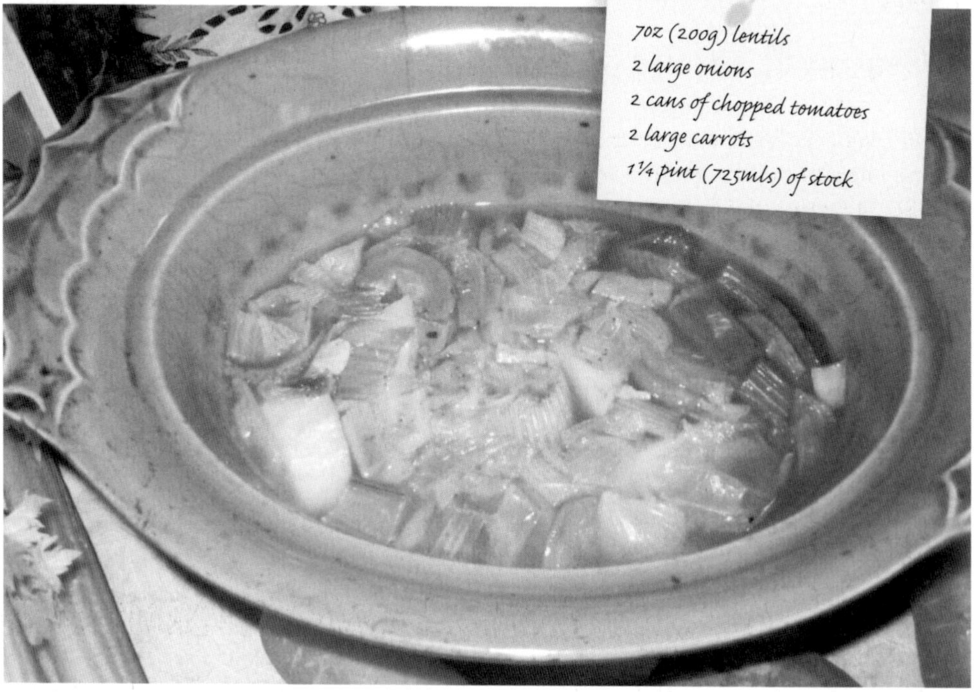

Lentil and carrot soup. (Photograph courtesy Ron and Barbara Strachan)

Method

- Sauté the sliced onion and chopped carrot and add rest of the ingredients to the pan.
- Simmer for 30 minutes until lentils are soft and well cooked.
- Whisk to a soft consistency.
- Serve hot with garlic bread.

CAMBORNE

In Truro, Newquay, St Agnes, St Mawes and St Austell, Cornish cream, fudge and saffron cake is available by post. I realised that saffron cake was an institution in this county and also in Devon. There appeared to be family secrets in its connection. I bought one in Camborne where the dialect is different from the coastal Cornish tongue, and 'saffron-cake chat' is more free. I was told that saffron threads, like spices, were much prized and expensive and used only for delicate dishes. To have a saffron cake conferred distinction. In Lancashire it seems to be vanilla pods that are prized.

Saffron Cake

Ingredients

2lbs (900g) flour
2oz (50g) mixed peel
1lb (450g) butter
8oz (225g) currants
4oz (110g) sugar
8oz (225g) sultanas
1oz (25g) yeast
½ pint (275ml) warm milk
A pinch of saffron (soaked in ½ cup of water)

Method

- Put the yeast to rise in a bowl with 1 teaspoon of the sugar.
- Rub the fat into the flour and when the yeast has risen, add this to the flour.
- Mix to a soft dough by hand (you may have to add a little more of the warm milk).
- As you mix, add the dried fruit and the saffron.
- Put the bowl in a warm place and let the dough rise for 1 hour.
- Place in floured cake tins and let the dough rise for a further 20 minutes.
- Bake at 180°C/gas mark 4 for 1 hour – cake should be an attractive golden colour.

CAMELFORD

The estuary of the River Camel is important to town and county as it offers the only entry into Cornwall through which tidal waters can flow inland. Broad and sheltered, it is covered with pleasure boats in summer, and surfing is enjoyed. At Pentire Point there are high cliffs. From a path which follows the abandoned railway line to Padstow are fine views of the River Camel. Camelford, 700ft above sea level, has a bridge dated 1521 and a camel for the town hall weathervane, which is merely a play on words, for the meaning is actually'beautiful, curved river with ford'.

Cherry Turnovers

Cherry turnovers were made in the days of annual cherry fairs when cherries were in great profusion in the vale of'Cherry Bounce'. Supposedly invented by a Cornish housewife, no specific recipe was forthcoming, but presented with a pound of luscious, stoned, washed cherries, the enterprising cook would surely make them like Coventry Godcakes, encased in squares of puff pastry, moistened at the edges and 'turned over' triangle-wise after putting a little sugar and moisture with the cherries.

Ingredients

FOR THE PUFF PASTRY: *(I was told that the butter has to be of the same consistency as the dough and that 'the top of a quick oven is best for puff pastry)*

8oz (225g) unsalted butter (lard, salted butter or margarine will not do)
8oz (225g) white flour, dried, with a pinch of salt
Cold water to mix
Lemon juice

Method

- ❖ Rub 1oz (25g) of butter into the flour. Make a well in the centre and squeeze in a few drops of lemon juice. Add a little water and mix to a dough which should be neither stiff nor sticky.
- ❖ Knead the dough until smooth and leave in a cool place.
- ❖ Roll out the dough ¾in thick.
- ❖ Put the whole of the butter on it evenly in small 'dabs'.
- ❖ Fold into three and give a turn to the left. Roll out evenly. After which, place the dough on a plate and leave in 'a cold a place as possible'.

Choux Pastry

Ingredients

2½oz (60g) flour
1¾oz (55g) margarine
¾ pint (425ml) water
Pinch of salt
2 eggs

Method

- ❖ Put the margarine and water in a pan and melt. Bring to the boil.
- ❖ Remove from the heat, stir in the flour.
- ❖ Return to the heat, beating until the mixture thickens.
- ❖ Remove from the heat and cool slightly.

Chocolate Eclairs

- ❖ Grease baking sheets.
- ❖ Put choux pastry (made as in above recipe) into a forcing bag and pipe into lengths onto the baking sheets.
- ❖ Bake at 220°C/gas mark 7 for 10 minutes, and then reduce heat to 190°C/gas mark 5 for a further 10 minutes.
- ❖ When cool, split and fill with cream and make the chocolate topping.

Ingredients

CHOCOLATE TOPPING FOR THE ECLAIRS

1oz (25g) cocoa
6oz (175g) icing sugar
½oz (10g) butter
2 tablespoons hot water

Method

- ❖ Place the water and butter in a pan and melt.
- ❖ Add the cocoa and mix until smooth.
- ❖ Sieve in the icing sugar, gently reheating to achieve a smooth consistency. Spread over each éclair.

CAPE CORNWALL

Pendeen Watch Lighthouse guides shipping between Cape Cornwall and Gurnard's Head with its beam of light, which can reach twenty miles away at sea. The area is strewn with prehistoric remains which lie amidst acres of heather and gorse.

A coastal path leads to Zennor along some fine scenery and mine workings, and there is a mineral and mining museum there where, on an organised cliff walk, you are told more about the history of Cornish mining. It is best to keep to the path for there are unsuspected clefts and holes above the mine workings.

However, it was the Levant Mine that was deepest, its shaft descending 2,000ft and its levels penetrating a mile beneath the Atlantic Ocean.

This is a recipe from the days when people had allotments and country lanes on their doorsteps.

Herb Beer

Most 'Cornish baskets' came from a basket-making industry at Heamoor near Penzance.

Ingredients

1 basket fresh young nettles, washed
1 basket fresh young parsley, washed
6 medium-sized potatoes, peeled
3lb (1.35kg) sugar
A thick slice of bread spread with yeast and cut into 4-6 pieces
2 gallons (6l) water

Method

- Place the nettles and parsley in a piece of muslin and tie into a bag. Place in a pan, cover, and boil with the potatoes for an hour.
- Place the sugar in a container and pour liquid over it.
- When cooled add the yeast spread on toast.
- Allow time for the yeast to work, then strain into a cask, bung up and leave for 6 months before bottling.

Herb Pasty

Ingredients

Handful of parsley, watercress or spinach, washed well
Handful of shallots or leeks, finely chopped
Handful of bacon rashers, cut into small pieces
Shortcrust pastry
1 egg, beaten

Method

- Chop and scald the parsley, watercress or spinach.
- Place the shallots or leeks and bacon on rounds of shortcrust pastry.
- Crimp each pasty except at one point and pour into this a small amount of beaten egg.
- Seal the pasties.
- Bake as usual.

CHACEWATER

Chacewater, situated in a valley between Truro and Redruth, is a pleasant, quiet village but was once linked with mining copper, tin, arsenic, lead and even silver. Chace means 'hunting' and indicates that the area was, long ago, the hunting ground of the lords of Cornwall.

The Redruth and Chacewater Railway never reached Chacewater despite being built for the mines of St Day, but it serves well as a cycle track passing Devoran and on to the coast.

Rook Pie

Ruth Spaceley, a great-grandmother, called it 'a rich gamey pie made in the days when people were poor.' Eels, elvers and woodpigeons were also put into pies. Eel pies are still made, proof that old recipes will survive if they are cheap, tasty and nourishing.

Conger Eel Pie

These are wise words from a Cornish cook who did not fuss about with kitchen scales:

> Two good sized eels stewed in mushrooms, parsley, onion with two glasses of sherry, a good dash of Worcester sauce and a good squeeze of lemon juice. Put in a pie dish, top with slices of hard-boiled egg and cover with pastry. Bake for half an hour at 160°C/gas mark 3.

The renowned Cornish chef Rick Stein, speaking about taste observed, 'Good cooking is respect for good, fresh food'.

CHARLESTOWN

In the eighteenth century, Charlestown was a small fishing village called Porthmear, but a local landowner transformed it when he constructed a harbour in the 1790s to handle pilchards, china clay, stone, tin, copper ore, coal, timber and lime. Things went well and schooners such as the *Earl of Pembroke* were busy, but a decline in trade resulted in the china-clay industry being the only survivor and indeed that continues today. Men pushed wagons loaded with clay to ships waiting in the dock below and supplied through a network of tunnels.

Charlestown today has a heritage centre and looks much as it did in its heyday with many fine ships and traditional craftsmen.

Ships such as *Carrie* have starred in the film productions of *Voyage of the Dawn Trader*, *Crusoe* and *Conquest of Paradise*.

Charlestown Harbour.

Chocolate Date Fingers

Method

- Grease a Swiss roll tin.
- Put water in pan and heat with the margarine until melted.
- Sieve the dry ingredients into the bowl, add the sugar and chopped dates.
- Add the syrup to the melted ingredients and return to gentle heat.
- Break the egg into a well in the dry ingredients and beat with a wooden spoon. Pour in the melted liquid and mix well with all the ingredients.
- Pour into a tin and bake at 180°C/gas mark 4, and bake for ½ hour.
- The date fingers can be cut while still hot, but not removed from the tin until cold.

Ingredients

6oz (175g) flour
2oz (30g) caster sugar
4oz (110g) dates, chopped and stoned
½ teaspoon baking powder
1oz (25g) cocoa
1oz (25g) margarine
1 tablespoon syrup
¼ pint (150ml) hot water
¼ teaspoon bicarbonate of soda
1 egg

DEVORAN

At the Devoran Church garden party, held annually, we always liked to buy a pot of Seville orange marmalade made from a recipe that came to Cornwall via Dorset long ago.

Steeping the oranges in halves overnight to soften and give full flavour seems to get the best results.

Devoran Regatta, 1990.

Devoran Orange Marmalade

Ingredients

10 Seville oranges
8 pints (4.5 litres) water
7lb (3.1kg) sugar

Method

- Pare the oranges thinly. Cut in half and squeeze out the juice. Remove pips and put them into a small muslin bag.
- Steep the orange halves and peel overnight in cold water.
- Next day boil the halves, the peel and the pips until tender (keeping the pips in the muslin bag).
- Allow to cool then remove all the pulp from the orange halves and discard the pith.
- Add the purée to the sugar and boil for 15 minutes, stirring frequently.
- Add the juice and boil until the setting point is reached.
- Discard the bag of pips.

Rich Parkin

Ingredients

1lb (450g) oatmeal
8oz (225g) butter
8oz (225g) lard
4oz (110g) sugar
2oz (50g) ground ginger
1lb (450g) syrup or treacle

Method

- Melt the fats together and mix with the syrup or treacle and dry ingredients, mixing all very well.
- Spread in greased tins and bake in a slow oven for 2 hours.
- When taken out of the oven, mark in portions with a knife and wait 3 days before eating.
- The cake improves with keeping, and is an instance of the old 'pound cake' principle.

FALMOUTH

From the days of Elizabeth I, salted fish was treated as in the following recipe:

> Salt the pilchards, removing heads. Next day, lay them in a barrel between layers of 'bay salt' inserting scatterings of bay leaves and lemon peel as you stack the fish. Fill the barrel and seal completely, all air to be excluded. Store in a cool cellar. Every week the barrel should be turned upside-down. In three months the salted fish is ready for eating.

Drying and smoking of fish were other ways of preserving the harvest, which, in the heyday of pilchards, arrived in shoals numbering millions. When the railway came, fish could be sent fresh and express to London's Billingsgate Market and elsewhere.

Falmouth Harbour.

FLUSHING

Dutch engineers built its sea walls and quays in the seventeenth century. There are handsome houses built by the sea captains of Falmouth for trade reached the West Indies and North America as Flushing developed as a port. The trading ship *Queen* was wrecked at Trefusis Point on its return from Spain in 1814. Stone steps lend atmosphere and like Devoran, Flushing holds an annual regatta.

4oz Gingerbread

Ingredients

4oz (110g) butter
4oz (110g) soft brown sugar
4oz (110g) black treacle
4oz (110g) self-raising flour
4oz (110g) wholemeal flour
2 teaspoons ginger
2 teaspoons cinnamon
4oz (110g) dried fruit
1 large, beaten egg
Chopped stem ginger (if desired, for topping)

Method

- Mix all the ingredients together and add enough beaten egg to give a dropping consistency.
- Pour into a square, floured and greased tin.
- The ginger flavour can be further increased by decorating the top with chopped stem ginger.
- Bake in a slow oven for 2 hours.

Easter Biscuits

In the days when the end of winter was followed with relief and rejoicing, these were served at Flushing with a posy of spring flowers to decorate the plate.

Ingredients

8oz (225g) plain flour
4oz (110g) unsalted butter
4oz (110g) caster sugar
3oz (75g) sultanas
Grated rind of half a lemon
1 egg

Method

- Cream the butter and sugar.
- Add the lemon rind.
- Gradually beat in the egg and flour, then work in the sultanas, producing a fairly stiff dough.
- Roll out this paste and cut into biscuit shapes with a metal cutter or the top of a wine glass dipped in flour.
- Bake at 170°C/gas mark 3-4, for 15 minutes.

FOWEY

When visiting Fowey you must learn to call it 'Foy' as in 'toy'. My relatives in Cornwall looked aghast when I innocently pronounced it as it looks. In the town, steep, narrow streets plunge down to a harbour full of yachts.The deep anchorage available has allowed sea-going vessels such as the *Queen Elizabeth II* liner to call here.

The Ship Inn was once the fifteenth-century home of the Rashleigh family and the Lugger Inn goes back to the seventeenth century. History tells of the Fowey Gallants, more pirates than sailors, who troubled the French nation so much that they burnt Fowey down in 1457 and inspired Daphne Du Maurier's novel *Frenchman's Creek*.

Fowey, 1902. (Photograph courtesy Mr Orchard of St Austell)

Figgy Pudding with Cornish Burnt Cream

Ingredients

2oz (50g) self-raising flour
4oz (110g) suet
2 ripe figs, chopped well
2 teaspoons allspice
1 tablespoon sherry
4oz (110g) breadcrumbs
8oz (225g) seedless raisins
Grated rind of 1 lemon
2 eggs beaten with a little milk

Method

- Mix all the dry ingredients together.
- Stir in the eggs and sherry and add just enough milk to make a soft dough.
- Place in a buttered pudding dish and cover with two thicknesses of greaseproof paper, allowing room for the pudding to swell.
- Steam for 3½ hours.
- Serve hot with sherry sauce or burnt Cornish cream.

GLENDURGAN AND COME TO GOOD

The typically Cornish gardens of Glendurgan lie in a steep cleft running down to the sea, ideal for tropical plants. Given to the National Trust in 1962, they feature a maze, popular with the Victorians in the early nineteenth century and still enjoyed by visitors, although the house itself is not open. Reaching the sea you find a tiny hamlet, Durgan.

As for Come to Good, here we have a wonderful time capsule, unique, as only the Quakers (Society of Friends) could provide.

Catherine and her late husband, Eddie, in Glendurgan Gardens, July 1993.

Glendurgan Flaky Pastry

Ingredients

8oz (225g) flour
6oz (175g) margarine
cold water
¼ teaspoon finely ground sea salt

Method

- Sieve the flour and salt taking ¼ of the margarine to rub into the flour.
- Roll into a rectangle.
- Take another ¼ of the margarine and spread knobs of it over the pastry.
- Fold into 3.
- Roll and repeat this process until all margarine is worked into the pastry.

Liver Patties

From Glendurgan came this recipe to use with the above pastry.

Ingredients

10oz (275g) flaky pastry (as above)
1 egg
1 onion
1 tablespoon breadcrumbs
8oz (225g) liver
1 egg yolk
1oz (25g) butter
3 dessertspoons brandy

Method

- Wash and chop the liver and sauté in a pan.
- Chop the onion finely and add to the liver. Cook gently.
- Add the egg and yolk, beaten, the breadcrumbs and some seasoning.
- Fill pastry cases in patty tins and add lids.
- Brush with egg and milk.
- Bake at 220°C/gas mark 7 for 30 minutes.
- Pour a small quantity of brandy into each patty.

GWEEK

Gweek was a busy little port for hundreds of years, and it became Helston's main sea link, because the Rover Cober became blocked with sand. Timber, coal and lime were exchanged for tin and farm produce.

The well-known seal sanctuary at Gweek is where many oiled-up and injured seals are taken and have a chance of recovery on a good diet of fish and by a thorough clean after damage by tanker-oil spills.

The frigate *Anson* was wrecked on nearby Loe Bar when it was driven on to the sandbank in 1807. Although close to shore, 100 seamen died.

At nearby Glendurgan Gardens which reach down to the sea and are a handy bathing cove, we found a lovely spot for snacks and sandwiches, before going on to Trebah for the rest of the day.

The Seal Sanctuary at Gweek.

Jam Crunch Pie

Ingredients

Quantity of shortcrust pastry
Thick jam
2oz (50g) sugar
2oz (50g) butter
3oz (75g) flour

Gweek crunch pie. (Photograph courtesy Ron and Barbara Strachan)

Method

- Line a pie dish with the pastry.
- Cover with thick jam.
- Mix sugar, butter and flour together until it looks like breadcrumbs.
- Scatter over the jam and bake in a moderate oven.

HELSTON

One of the four stannary towns for the tin industry, Helston goes back to the days of King John (Cornish tin was checked for purity). Famous for its 'Furry Dance' every May, visitors join in the fun following the town band through the streets. Its ancient origin lies in welcoming the spring solstice.

This recipe was given to me from a lady who lived in Stithians, whose mother was once head dairymaid to Viscount Clifden at Lanhydrock.

Bacon curing was done in the farms and cottages using sacks of sawdust, 4*d* each from Sawyers. The flitches of bacon were hung in the wood smoke which gave a distinctive flavour.

Bacon and Beef Oggin

Method

- Roll out a round of thick pastry. Make a well in the centre into which crack a fresh egg.
- Around these arrange pieces of bacon and finely chopped beef.
- Crimp edges together and seal well.
- Cook as for Cornish pasty on a baking sheet.

KING HARRY FERRY

At King Harry Passage on the River Fal, a ferry has run for centuries, but where did the name originate? There are many stories, one popular version being that Henry VIII spent his honeymoon with Anne Boleyn at St Mawes Castle and there he signed a charter for the ferry to operate. However, as it was the same king that had castles built at St Mawes and Pendennis to protect the River Fal and other estuaries (it was Henry VIII that ordered Martello Towers for coastal defence), this link with his name rather discounts the romantic notion.

It was in 1888, the year my mother, Ethel Fielden, was born, that a soldier from Carclew tried to run a steam-driven ferry across the river instead of the old barge which had to be propelled by oars.

Restronguet Creek.

Actually a steam engine was not used for propulsion until 1956 when Ferry No. 4 was converted to steam.

When we eat the Ferryman's Wife Chocolate Cake, a recipe brought north by our granddaughter, King Harry is not thought of, only Cornish cream.

King Harry Ferry with ferrymen's cottages behind.

The Ferryman's Wife's Chocolate Cake and Cornish Cream

Ingredients

4oz (110g) self-raising flour
4oz (110g) butter
4oz (110g) caster sugar
1oz (25g) golden syrup
2 eggs
2 tablespoons cocoa
½ teaspoon vanilla essence
4 teaspoons of fresh milk
½ pint fresh double cream or Cornish clotted cream

Method

- Sift flour and cocoa.
- Cream butter, sugar, syrup and essence together until a pale colour and it is light in texture.
- Beat in the eggs one at a time, adding one tablespoon of the dry ingredients with each egg.
- Fold in the milk and remaining dry ingredients with a metal spoon.
- Transfer to a deep, round 8in cake tin. Smooth top level with a knife.
- Bake at 180°C/gas mark 4 for 40 minutes.
- Turn onto a wire cooling tray and leave to cool completely.
- Cut cake into 2 or 3 layers and fill with the double cream.

Venison Steaks

Method

- Melt butter in a large frying pan and cook the venison steaks.
- Remove the steaks and keep warm.
- Fry the apple slices and mix together the cream, whisky, juniper and honey.
- Add these to the pan and heat gently until warm.
- Pour this over the steaks and garnish with parsley.

Ingredients

4 venison steaks
1oz (25g) butter
2 cored, sliced eating apples
2 tablespoons whisky
1 teaspoon honey
¼ pint (150ml) fresh double cream
5 crushed juniper berries
Sprigs of parsley

KEA

Embowered in thick woodland and approached by narrow lanes is the ancient church of Kea. You think you will never arrive but when you do, kindness is overwhelming. We had one sermon based on the film *Chocolat* which made us think, as did a visit on another occasion from 'Bishop Bill'.

Cornish cream calls for chocolate. It is a winner in the Ferryman's Wife's Chocolate Cake (see King Harry Ferry), and although some tough mariners turn their noses up at salads, they will tolerate the following recipe.

The youth group from St Kea Church on their annual weekend gathering at Land's End.

Cherry Chocolate

Method

- Line a square tin with lightly buttered greaseproof paper.
- Place the butter in a basin and melt over a pan of hot water.
- Sieve the sugar into a basin with the drinking chocolate and add to the melted butter.
- Keep stirring.
- Remove from the heat and add the beaten egg yolk immediately, then the evaporated milk.
- Pour a layer of mixture over the bottom of the tin.
- Cover with a layer of biscuits and continue to add layers ending with some chocolate mixture.
- Chill in the fridge for 1 hour and decorate with cherries.

Ingredients

6oz (175g) butter
8oz (225g) icing sugar
1 egg yolk
3oz (75g) drinking chocolate
3 tablespoons evaporated milk
4oz (110g) glacé cherries
8oz (225g) oblong-shaped biscuits

From Come to Good, the ancient home of the Quakers, came the following recipe.

Old Fashioned Broth

The custom was to have the broth first, then the beef with boiled potatoes. Any beef left over was eaten cold and said to be quite delicious for sandwiches.

Method

- For 3 to 4 days, rub the beef with salt.
- Put into a saucepan with the carrots, onion, turnip and leek and cook for about 2 hours. The cabbage can go in towards the end of the cooking.

Ingredients

3lb (1.35kg) brisket of beef
Salt to taste
4oz (110g) Carrots, chopped
4oz (110g) Onion, chopped
4oz (110g) Turnip, diced
4oz (110g) Leek, chopped
4oz (110g) Curly green cabbage, chopped

Kiddly (or Kettle Broth)

This soup was eaten on cold nights, poured over squares of stale homemade bread.

Ingredients

3 onions
1 thick rasher of bacon
Pepper
2oz (50g) dripping

Method

- Peel and cut up the onions and simmer for an hour with the bacon.
- Add a dash of pepper and the dripping.
- Sieve.

KILLIOW PARK

Large houses like Killiow once had about thirty horses and the blacksmiths were kept busy. It was Dickie Dunstan's job and his tools are still on display. As we walked around the park we saw Duchess and Princess, two heavy Shire horses. Both assisted with farm work such as chain harrowing grassland or hauling timber. Every evening they were put out to pasture, a splendid sight, a piece of old England indeed.

Mushroom Soup

Ingredients

1lb (450g) fresh wild or cultivated mushrooms
1 clove garlic
1 small onion
1 bunch parsley
1½ pints (845ml) good stock
Juice of 1 lemon

Mushroom soup. (Photograph courtesy Claire Forbes)

Method

- Cook the ingredients gently in butter until soft.
- Add the stock and the lemon juice.
- Simmer for 15 minutes.
- Add a tablespoon of cream just before serving.

Killiow Apple Cake

Ingredients

8oz (225g) self-raising flour
½ level teaspoon of bicarbonate of soda
4oz (110g) butter or margarine
6oz (175g) sugar
2 Bramley apples, grated
6oz (175g) sultanas
2 eggs, beaten

Method

- Sift in the flour and bicarbonate of soda.
- Rub the butter into the mixture.
- Add the sugar, apples and sultanas.
- Stir well and then add the eggs.
- Bake for approximately 1½ hours at 180°C/gas mark 4.

LAMORNA

Lamorna Cove is a place of history and legend, and one of our favourite places that we visited on our honeymoon in 1950.

There is a mermaid rock where merry maidens were turned into stone because they danced on the Sabbath.

Poached Salmon with Lemon Mayonnaise

Ingredients

Salmon
4 egg yolks
2 dessertspoons white vinegar
1 level teaspoon powdered mustard
Sea salt and freshly milled white peppercorns
¾ pint (425ml) sunflower oil
The juice and zest of two lemons

Old recipes used anchovies, horseradish, capers and walnut pickle to serve with salmon and the fish was once very plentiful. In 1875 its price, considered very high, reached 1*s* per lb.

Little accompaniment is actually necessary, except lemon, but this lemon mayonnaise makes a change and can be made with an electric mixer, easier than in the days of yore.

Method

- Place salmon in cold, salted water. Bring to the boil, then simmer, allowing 5 minutes per lb.
- Allow the salmon to lie in the liquor.
- Blend together egg yolks, vinegar, mustard and seasoning.
- When well-mixed, trickle in the oil, at a slow, gradual rate, increasing the rate of flow as the mayonnaise thickens.
- Add the lemon juice and zest.

A Marinade for Bream, Salmon or Trout

Ingredients

3 fish, whole or in steaks
1 onion
1 bay leaf
¼ pint (150ml) white vinegar
½ teaspoon ground cinnamon
½ teaspoon ground cloves
1 lemon
1 sprig of rosemary
Freshly-ground sea salt
¾ pint (425ml) white wine
Flour and oil for the fish

Method

- Dredge the fish with the flour and brown in the hot oil.
- Reduce the heat and cook for around 10 minutes.

Sweet Sauce (if there be no cream)

Ingredients

1 pint (570ml) fresh milk
3 egg yolks
The rind of 1 lemon
A little sugar

Method

- Put the milk into a pan with the lemon rind and bring to boiling point.
- Strain over the well-beaten egg yolks.
- Pour back into pan but do not boil.
- Sweeten to taste.

Simple Sauce

Ingredients

1 teaspoon butter
1 breakfast cup of milk and water combined
A little grated nutmeg
1 dessertspoon cornflour
1 dessertspoon brown sugar

Method

- Mix all ingredients together and stir until mixture boils.
- Cook for a few minutes, continually stirring for smoothness sake.

Mint and Apple Chutney

We found this chutney useful up to and beyond Christmas, especially after a poor summer had left a harvest of green tomatoes.

Ingredients

1lb (450g) cooking apples, cored and finely chopped
1lb (450g) sultanas
1lb (450g) onions, minced
1lb (450g) green tomatoes, sliced
1lb (450g) sugar
1 pint (570ml) malt vinegar
1oz (25g) ginger root
1 bunch fresh mint, minced

Method

- ❖ Mix together all the ingredients in a stainless-steel pan.
- ❖ Cook for 45 minutes, stirring initially until the sugar has dissolved, and for time to time as the chutney simmers and softens.
- ❖ Remove the ginger root.
- ❖ Pot into warm jars.

LAND'S END

These days the Land's End signpost is a favourite spot to be photographed.

Grace Thomas ran Penwith House from 1902 to 1906, a time when there was a Penzance to Land's End horse-bus service.

Now there is a shipwreck adventure playground, but nothing can diminish the drama of the Armed Knight Rocks. The Romans called it 'Belerion', the sea of storms. England's First and Last Hotel serves delicious seafood but nothing tastes better than a Cornish pasty whilst sitting on those beetling cliffs, looking out to sea. Peter de Savary, who owned both Land's End and John O' Groats, said, 'Nothing between you but Newfoundland and 3,000 miles of restless ocean'.

Land's End, *c.* 1932. The Longships Lighthouse was built in 1794.

Cockle Soup

This is a very old recipe. Make sure that the cockles come from an unpolluted source.

Ingredients

2oz (50g) butter
2 pints (1.21 litre) cockles, scrubbed and well rinsed
1 bay leaf
½ pint (275ml) thin cream
2oz (50g) flour
2½ pints (1.5litres) cockle stock
Ground sea salt and pepper
2 tablespoons chopped parsley

Method

- Place cockles in a large pan in enough salted water to cover. Add a dessertspoon of salt and 1¾ pints (1 litre) water.
- Bring to the boil and the cockles will open.
- Allow to cool, then remove from their shells.
- Strain and reserve the cockle stock. Melt butter in another pan and add the flour, cook for two minutes.
- Stirring all the time, add the strained cockle stock and the bay leaf.
- Simmer for 10 minutes, then sir in the cream and seasoning.
- Add the cockles and parsley. Heat but do not boil.

LANHYDROCK

150,000 people from around the world visit Lanhydrock, mostly between April and October annually, and one may wonder why, for it lies in a lonely part of Cornwall. The reason is Lanhydrock House, standing in 900 acres and one of the finest country houses in Britain.

On the site of a monastery which had belonged to St Petroc's Priory in Bodmin, a house was built between 1642 and 1644. Baron Robartes lived there, planting the lovely avenue of sycamores in 1648. The River Fowey is nearby.

A great fire in 1881 wrought terrible damage but refurbishments were made and by 1953 the National Trust took over maintenance of Lanhydrock House. A hearty meal can be had from the restaurant there, located in the former stables and coach house.

Gatehouse at Lanydrock.

Lanhydrock Leeky Pie

Method

- Wash the leeks by splitting down the middle and separating layers where sand may have lodged, then cut into small pieces and cook rapidly.
- Dice the bacon and sauté in butter.
- Beat the cream and eggs together and pour over the drained leeks.
- Cover with the flaky pastry lid and bake at 180°C/ gas mark 4 for 20 minutes.

Ingredients

12 leeks
8oz (225g) bacon
¼ pint (150ml) cream
2 eggs
Flaky pastry, sufficient to cover pie

Cornish Christmas Cake

The scene on Christmas Eve in castles of old, like St Mawes and Pendennis, was described in this account from Carisbrook Castle in 1606:

In the great hall, antlers of deer from the forest adorned walls, above floated rosemary, bays, evergreens, banners, holly. Faggots in heaps lay in readiness on the hearth with its andiron bar, fire dogs to support the burning wood. There was music and shouting and the appointed 'Lord of Misrule', clad in quaint habit and followed by officials would shout, 'Come bring with a noise, my merry boys, the Christmas log to the firing'.

The brand that was quenched last Christmas was relit by the steward and applied to the heap of faggots, 'Be Merry! Drink success to the firing'. Spicy, nut-brown ale was drunk, with roasted apples in it and carried in on 'Christmas lambswool'. 'Hand back, here be the mummers'. A burly figure with a long white beard, carrying a staff, crowned with holly and dressed in sheepskins roared, 'Would you keep me out; Christmas, old Christmas?'

The first course and the principal dish was boar's head. On Christmas morn the Yule log still burned. Apparently it took twenty men to carry it.

Cornish Christmas cake. (Photograph courtesy Ron and Barbara Strachan)

Method

- All the above ingredients must be kept in a lidded container to which 6 tablespoons of brandy have been added. Shake every day for 2 weeks.

Ingredients *(for stage 1)*

8oz (225g) raisins
10oz (275g) sultanas
4oz (110g) mixed peel
4oz (110g) currants
5oz (150g) cherries
2oz (50g) almonds, chopped
2oz (50g) Brazil nuts, chopped
1 level teaspoon ground cinnamon
1 level teaspoon mixed spice

Ingredients *(for stage 2)*

6oz (175g) butter
8oz (225g) dark muscavado sugar
8oz (225g) plain flour
3 eggs
2 level teaspoons black treacle
½ teaspoon baking powder
The grated rind of 1 lemon and 1 small orange

Method

- Cream the butter and muscovado sugar.
- Mix in the beaten egg, whisking well.
- Fold in the flour with the baking powder. Add the treacle, lemon and orange rind and finally the fruit mixture.
- Mix well and turn into a greased, lined 8in cake tin.
- Bake at 135-150°C/gas mark 1-2 for 3¼ hours.

LAUNCESTON

Launceston used to guard the main way into Cornwall and Devon with its thirteenth-century castle, now in ruins. It was once used as a prison; George Fox, the Quaker leader was imprisoned there for handing out religious pamphlets in St Ives. Public hangings were held on the castle green.

At the White Hart Inn they may have served West Country Bacon Pie.

Launceston Castle.

West Country Bacon Pie

Method

- Soak bacon for an hour in cold water and then drain.
- Arrange the slices of apples, onions and potatoes with the bacon in a large pie dish.
- Pour over the stock.
- Roll out the pastry and make a lid to fit the pie dish. Brush with beaten egg and make a hole in for the steam to escape.
- Bake at 230°C/gas mark 8 for 15 minutes. Reduce heat to 160°C/gas mark 3 for 1½ hours.

Ingredients

8oz (225g) baking apples, peeled and sliced
1 small onion, peeled and sliced
1lb (450g) unsmoked back bacon, chopped
12oz (350g) potatoes, peeled and sliced
½ pint (275ml) stock
1 beaten egg
8-10oz (225-300g) shortcrust pastry depending on thickness of crust required

Soused Herring

Salads have had scant mention in Cornwall where people seem to prefer meat and fish. One brawny fisherman told me 'we are not rabbits', and explained how to prepare soused herring. I think a green salad would be a welcome accompaniment.

Method

- Split the fish and place a bay leaf inside each.
- Lay in an ovenproof dish.
- Sprinkle with the sugar and peppercorns and cover with the vinegar.
- Cover and bake at 180°C/gas mark 4 for 1 hour.
- Allow to cool.

Ingredients

8 herrings
16 black peppercorns
½ pint (275ml) white vinegar
8 bay leaves
1 teaspoon brown sugar

LELANT

Once a prosperous port, now sand choked by the River Hayle, driven by gales. It even has buried houses. On the edge of the sand dunes stands a fifteenth-century church dedicated to St Uny. This part of the long-distance coastal path calls for walkers to use the ferry in order to cross the estuary.

Honey Madeira cake. (Photograph courtesy Ron and Barbara Strachan)

Honey Madeira Cake

Method

- Cream the butter with the honey and sugar until soft and pale.
- Mix in the lemon rind and beat in the eggs, adding a little flour to prevent curdling.
- Sift the flour over the mixture and fold it in gently.
- Put the mixture into a greased and well-lined loaf tin.
- Bake at 160°C/gas mark 3 for 1¼ hours.
- Cool on a wire rack and glaze with the warmed, clear honey and sprinkle with the toasted almonds.

Ingredients

FOR THE CAKE

9oz (250g) self-raising flour
6oz (175g) butter
4oz set honey (110g)
3oz (75g) caster sugar
Grated rind of 1 lemon
3 eggs, lightly beaten

FOR THE GLAZE

1 tablespoon clear honey
2 tablespoons blanched almonds, toasted and chopped

Looe

Looe is situated seven miles from Liskeard on the steep banks of the River Looe. East and West Looe are connected by a bridge and face each other across the harbour. The town exported Cornish granite and the stone was used to build Westminster Bridge and the London Embankment.

Entrance to Looe Harbour, *c.* 1953.

Higher Chapel Street, East Looe, *c.* 1953.

The bridge and East Looe, *c.* 1953.

Spiced Whisky Cake

This party cake from Looe was brought home by my brother after he had cycled all the way there from Lancashire at a time when there were no cars on the roads because of petrol rationing.

Method

- Grease and line an 8in straight-sided cake tin.
- Cream the margarine and sugar.
- Put the raisins in a pan with the water and bring to the boil. Simmer for 15 minutes.
- Beat the egg into the creamed mixture.
- Sieve in the dry ingredients.
- Drain the raisins and make the liquid up to ¼ pint again, then add the whisky.
- Add the fruit, walnuts and liquid and stir well.
- Bake in the centre of the oven at 180°C/gas mark 4 for ¾ hour.

Ingredients

8oz (225g) seedless raisins
4oz (110g) soft margarine
1 egg
1 level teaspoon bicarbonate of soda
3oz (75g) walnut halves
¼ pint (150ml) water
5oz (150g) soft brown sugar
6oz (175) flour
½ teaspoon nutmeg
2 tablespoons whisky

LOSTWITHIEL

What's past the yellow door?
Who knocks?
No answer lay in waiting
But the tick of time,
That mocks magenta fuchsia,
Thrusting bee, clinging together
Murmuring rapturously,
Come to my honeyed door, perpetually.
Catherine Rothwell

I wrote these lines sitting in sunshine at St Agnes after climbing up to the Beacon, which was waiting to be lit again to commemorate the victory of the English when the Spanish Armada attempted invasion. We were there 400 years later and I remember the very hot sunshine and the scents of lavender, fuchsia and valerian mingled to produce a moment I never forgot. Years later this poem won a prize in a literary competition which launched me on a writing career and led to three more literary awards (not for poetry).

Honey, a wonderful food, is used in many Cornish recipes. Like salt, it has been indispensable for centuries.

Before the Reformation, the monks respected and understood the ways of bees. Brother Adam of Buckfast Abbey was still caring for bees at the apiary when he was aged ninety. Indeed, honey bees are associated with longevity, a belief strongly held by the late Dame Barbara Cartland, the well-known romantic novelist

Honey Butter

Heat gently a quantity of unsalted butter until soft. Blend in an equal amount of Cornish Honey. Keep in an earthenware pot and use as a spread on wholemeal bread.

Schoolboys William Pye and Bernard Houghton tend the honeycombs and bees during the Second World War at Lostwithiel.

Honey Cream Sauce

Method

- Whip the cream, stir in the honey and lemon juice.
- Whip well and place in a glazed, earthenware pot.
- Use fresh, chilled summer fruits such as plums, apricots, redcurrants, raspberries.

Ingredients

1 tablespoon lemon juice
6 tablespoons honey
6oz (175g) double cream

THE LIZARD

Brawn, a classic medieval food, was served with mustard and Malmsey or the sweetest of Madeiras. The secret of its flavour lies in long simmering. Although whole pigs' heads were boiled for this recipe, a more convenient way is followed. This brawn is delicious accompanied with a fresh, crunchy green salad, and wine of course. Malmsey wine is mentioned as early as 1478 when the Duke of Clarence was said to have drowned in a butt of Malmsey wine in the Tower. In the reign of Henry VIII, an Act of Parliament forbade it to be sold for more than 12*d* a gallon.

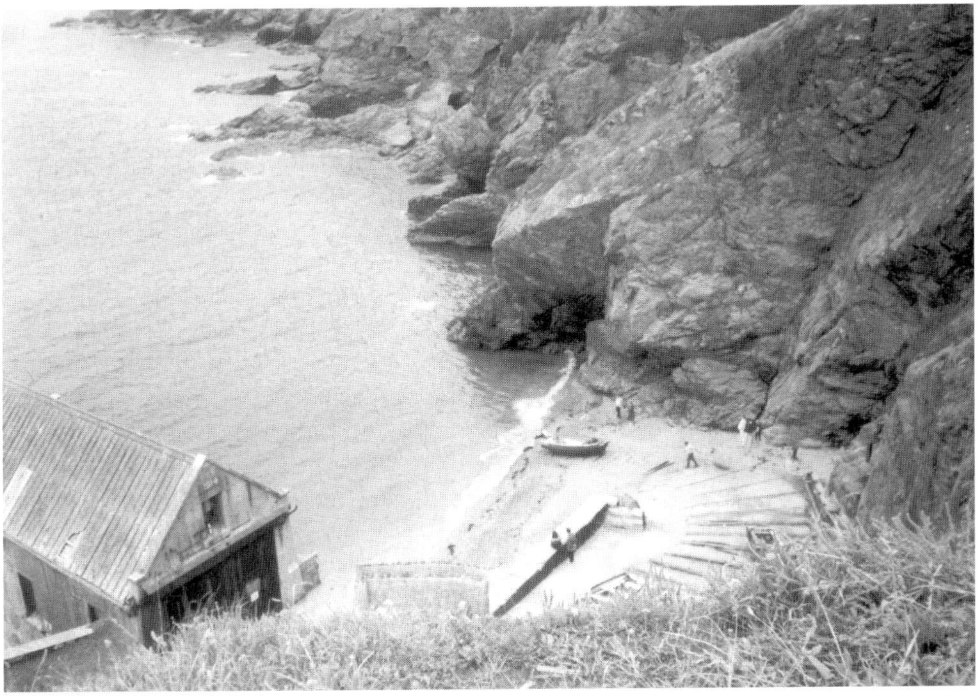

A small cove on the Lizard peninsula.

Brawn

Method

- ❖ Place all ingredients in a saucepan and cover with water.
- ❖ Cook for 4 hours, simmering slowly.
- ❖ Allow to cool.
- ❖ Remove meat from bones and place in a mould or pudding basin.
- ❖ Strain the stock over the meat and leave on a cold pantry shelf to set.

Ingredients

8oz (225g) shin beef
1 cow heel
8oz (225g) ham or oxtail
2 small onions, chopped
A bunch of herbs tied in muslin
4 peppercorns
4 cloves
2 bay leaves

Macaroons

Method

- ❖ Add the sugar to the flour.
- ❖ Rub in the margarine and bind with egg yolk.
- ❖ Roll out the shortcake into an oblong and raise a ½in strip around each edge, pressing with the fingers to pattern the edge (gimping).
- ❖ Spread with jam.
- ❖ Whip up the egg white, add the sugar and ground almonds.
- ❖ Spread this mixture on the jam.
- ❖ Bake at 160°C/gas mark 3 for about 25 minutes.

Ingredients

FOR THE SHORTCAKE
4oz (110g) self-raising flour
3oz (75g) margarine
1oz (25g) sugar

FOR THE FILLING
2oz (50g) sugar
2oz (50g) ground almonds
A little jam
1 egg yolk
1 egg white

MARAZION

Maggie Satterthwaite's Cornish Pasty

We were first introduced to Maggie's pasties one August fifty years ago, at St Winifred's House, Marazion, where we spent our honeymoon. The perfect follow-up to her pasties was the most mouth-watering fruit salad we have ever tasted. Maggie's husband had a fruit shop and she was used to feeding commandos. That fortnight was a good start to married life.

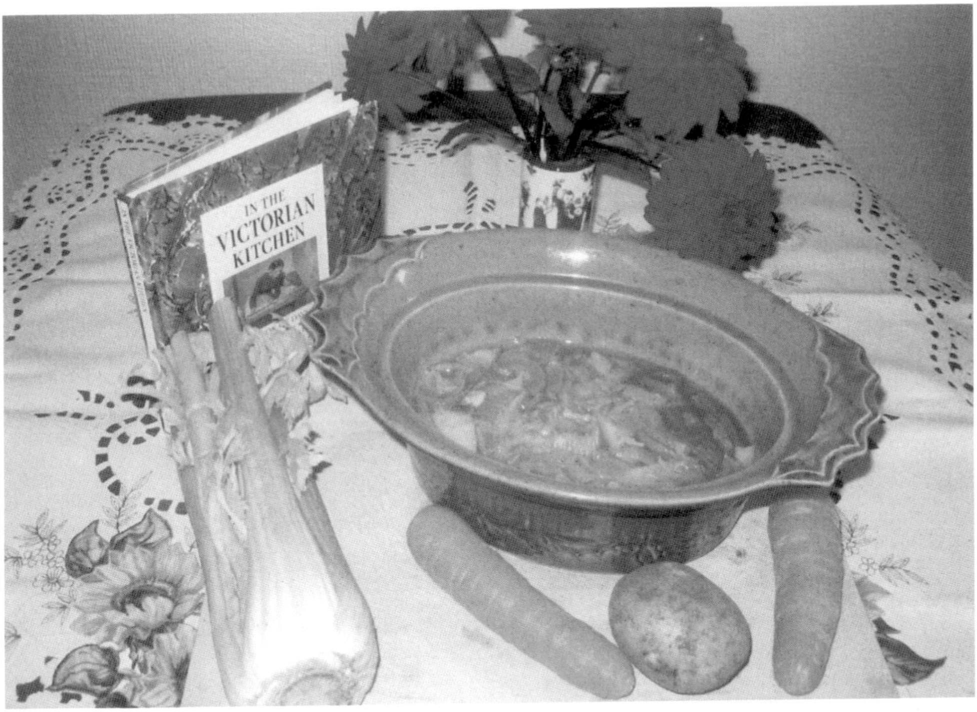

Carrot, celery and potato are alternative ingredients for a Cornish pasty. (Photograph courtesy Ron and Barbara Strachan)

Method

- Make the pastry by rubbing the fat into the flour until it resembles breadcrumbs.
- Add the seasoning and gradually bind with water.
- Roll out, not too thinly, to form rounds the size of a dinner plate.
- Gently lift one half of the pastry round with a rolling pin and spread the filling evenly from one end to the other, allowing room at the edge for sealing and firm closure.
- Moisten one half of the pastry circle with water and fold over to meet the other half.
- Seal well by pressing the edges of the pastry together, starting at the middle, with a crimping action (practice makes perfect).
- Place the pasties on a baking sheet, glazing the tops with milk or beaten egg for a golden look.
- Cook at 200°/gas mark 6 for 25 minutes then lower to 170°/gas mark 3-4 for a further 10 minutes.

Ingredients

FOR THE PASTRY

1lb (450g) strong white flour
8oz (225g) soft margarine
Freshly ground salt and pepper
Water to mix

FOR THE FILLING

1½oz (40g) onion, finely chopped
4oz (110g) chuck steak, finely diced
6oz (175g) potatoes finely sliced
2oz (50g) turnip, finely chopped
Knob of butter
Ground sea salt and pepper

Apricot Jam

Ingredients

3lb (1.35kg) fresh apricots
3lb (1.35kg) granulated sugar
½ pint (275ml) water
Grated rind of 1 lemon
3oz (75g) split almonds

Method

- Wash the fruit, removing stalks and leaves, halve and stone.
- Place fruit, water and lemon in a pan and cook until tender.
- Remove from heat and dissolve the sugar in the pan.
- Bring to the boil and continue until setting point is reached, but do not overboil.
- Add the halved almonds. Pot and cover in sterilised warm jars.

MEVAGISSEY

An ancient fishing port established in the Middle Ages, its steep and narrow streets attract crowds in summer. Its harbours, inner and outer, were developed in the eighteenth and nineteenth centuries as a haven for a large fleet which were mainly engaged in fishing for pilchards. The fish were cured and exported as far as Italy. Locally the pilchard was referred to as 'Mevagissey Duck!' Mousehole, Newlyn and other Cornish ports called pilchards 'Fair Maids.' There must have been much lamentation when this fish decided to leave Cornwall for good.

Mevagissy, *c.* 1961. (Photograph courtesy J. Salmon Ltd, Sevenoaks)

Mackerel with Gooseberries

Presumably the tartness of the gooseberries tempered the oiliness of this nourishing and tasty fish.

Ingredients

6 Mackerel
3oz (75g) sugar
4oz (110g) butter
1lb (450g) gooseberries, topped and tailed
Pinch of nutmeg
Parsley and seasoned flour

Method

- Roll the fish in the seasoned flour and cook in the butter in a large frying pan.
- Stew the gooseberries in water and sugar.
- Serve with the tender mackerel along with the pinch of nutmeg and chopped parsley.

MORWENSTOW

Close to the Cornish coastal path and not far from Bude is Morwenstow, worth collecting a recipe from if only because in the nineteenth century its vicar, Revd Robert Stephen Hawker, played practical jokes on his congregation. He could be serious too, because he roundly condemned the plundering of the wrecked ships, a common tempting practice on such a dangerous, stormy coast. He also originated the Harvest Festivals in churches. He wrote poems in a driftwood hut he had constructed and his best joke was to dress up as a mermaid, sit on a rock by the seashore and wait for an audience. He then stood up and sang the national anthem. His best-known poem was the 'Song of the Western Men'.

Bilberry Jam

As with rowan, redcurrant, rosehip and other jellies, this jam was used sparingly with meats such as rabbit, venison and lamb.

Ingredients

3½lb bilberries
2lb (900g) sugar
¼ pint water
¼oz tartaric acid

Method

- Wash the berries and stew with the tartaric acid until tender.
- Add the sugar and bring to the boil. Simmer until it sets, although this fruit will never set very firm.

MOUSEHOLE

Baked Pilchards

Mousehole was once the centre of Cornwall's pilchard fishing industry. The pilchards, however, left these shores around the turn of the twentieth century which was bad enough, but worse was the loss of the Penlee lifeboat and its entire crew, all Mousehole men.

Ingredients

4 clean, boned pilchards
2 cups thin cream
2 eggs
2 tablespoons chopped parsley

Method

- Beat the eggs, cream and parsley.
- Pour over the pilchards and bake for 30 minutes at 180°C/gas mark 4.

This is how pilchards were prepared in Newquay but when the shoals of pilchards went, pollock, plaice and mackerel replaced them. St Ives Fisheries displayed a good variety; megrin, dabs, cod fillets, ray, mackerel, smoked haddock, whiting, shrimps and prawns all offered scope for good cooks.

Beef Olives

Ingredients

1lb (450g) steak
½ slice of dry bread
4oz (110g) finely minced suet
Salt and pepper
Small quantity of beef stock

Method

- Cut the steak into thin pieces.
- Crumb the dry bread and mix with salt and pepper and finely minced suet.
- Make this into a firm paste, using a little cold water.
- Spread this on the slices of steak and roll up on a long beef skewer.
- Brown the meat in butter and add some beef dripping or beef stock, preferably made from bones.
- Cover and cook at 200°C/gas mark 6 for 1½ hours, keeping rolls well basted.

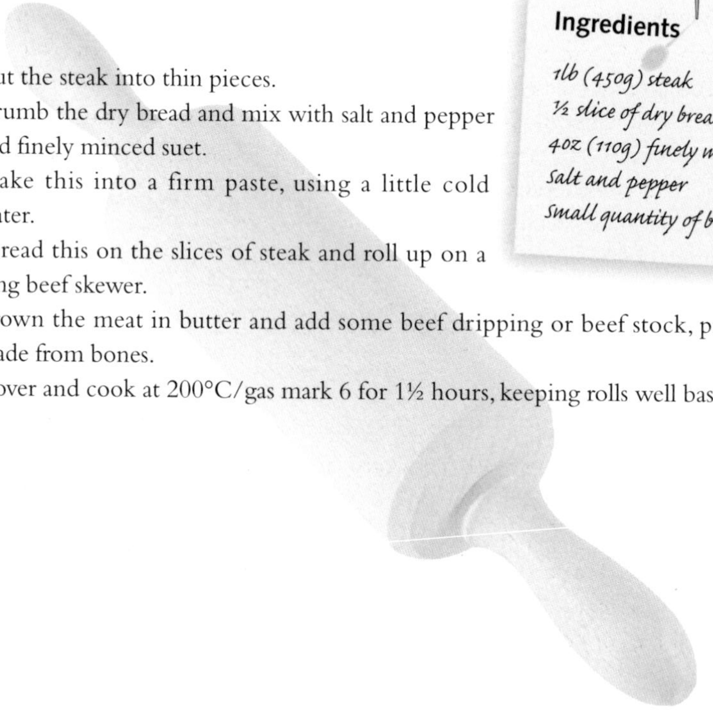

Mince Mould

Ingredients

2lb (900g) lean, minced steak
2oz (50g) chopped bacon
2oz (50g) breadcrumbs
1 egg yolk
¼ pint (150ml) beef stock
chopped parsley

Method

- Put the minced steak in a bowl and add the bacon and chopped parsley.
- Mix this with breadcrumbs and egg yolk.
- Add the beef stock, season to taste and mix all well.
- Butter an earthenware mould and press in the mixture.
- Cover with buttered paper and put in a saucepan containing about 3in boiling water.
- Steam for 2 hours, topping up the water when necessary.
- Allow to cool.
- Serve the mince mould with a green salad or watercress and sliced tomatoes.

Boiled Lobster

My elder brother and his wife spent their honeymoon at the Lobster Pot in Mousehole at the beginning of the Second World War, when lobsters were plentiful and a much appreciated delicacy in those ration-book days. They enjoyed the shellfish in its simple form as served for years past. By 1988 and spoiled for choice there were lobster soufflés, sauces and thermidors prominent on hotel menus.

Grilled salmon from the River Camel was another of their favourite treats. Many years ago salmon was considered ordinary – apprentices could ask their masters not to serve it more than twice a week. A whole salmon was cooked in a fish kettle (now a collector's item).

A boiled lobster was procurable by plunging a live lobster into 4 quarts of boiling water, in which had been placed 4 teaspoons of salt and a bunch of parsley. After 8 minutes the meat from the lobster was served with a sauce.

Sauce to Serve With Boiled Lobster

Ingredients

2 teaspoons mild mustard
2 tablespoons white vinegar
1 cup clotted Cornish cream
1 raw egg yolk
Salt and pepper
2 teaspoons sugar

Method

- Mix the egg yolk with the mustard, sugar and vinegar.
- Add seasoning.
- Fold in the clotted cream and stir very well to ensure smooth consistency.
- Serve with fresh-boiled lobster.

Salmon Steaks

Ingredients

Salmon steaks
Flour
Oatmeal
Knob of butter

Method

- Wash and pat dry the salmon steaks and dust with the flour mixed with oatmeal and salt and pepper.
- Grill in butter for 10 minutes, taking care not to overcook.
- Garnish with lemon slices and parsley sprigs.

This recipe is lovely served hot in springtime with pod peas and small new potatoes.

Star-Gazey Pie

The stormy, sea-tossed past of Mousehole and Mevagissey breathes pilchards. This recipe impressed me because I realised that Bob Timmins and his team of workmen were not joking entirely when they explained that the herring or mackerel heads are left on the fish and hang outside the pie, 'gazing' at the stars. Cornish cook Mrs Colwell said 'Make a slit in the pastry, making heads of the fish poke through'.

Ingredients

FOR THE FILLING

4 pilchards, herring or mackerel
1 tablespoon chopped parsley
The juice and rind of one lemon, finely grated
4 tablespoons fine breadcrumbs
2 sliced hard-boiled eggs
1 rasher bacon, chopped
1 chopped onion
Freshly ground sea salt and pepper
¼ pint (150ml) white wine

FOR THE FLAKY PASTRY

8oz (225g) plain flour
8oz (225g) lard
4 tablespoons cold water
Pinch of salt

Method

- Sieve flour and salt into a mixing bowl.
- Cut ½ of the hardened lard into 'chippings' and mix into the flour.
- Add the water very gradually to make a dough.
- Roll out pastry and place the remainder of the lard, cut into in small quantities, all over the rolled out pastry.
- At least 8 times fold over, roll out, fold again and roll out.
- Chill the pastry in a fridge and make a lid for your Star Gazey Pie.
- Clean and gut the fish but leave the heads on.
- Soak the breadcrumbs in the milk to make them swell.
- Add the lemon peel, ½ the onion, ½ the lemon juice and the parsley.
- Stuff each fish with this mixture and place in a deep pie dish with the heads of the fish hanging over the edge.
- Cover with the eggs and bacon and the remaining onion and lemon juice. Pour over the white wine.

- Roll the pastry out to size and cover, leaving the fish heads outside.
- Bake at 220°C/gas mark 7 for 20 minutes then at 180°C/gas mark 4 for a further 10 minutes.

Christmas calls for much variety in rich and unusual food, even down to the leftovers when the great feast is past. One of the most unusual must be that served at Mousehole. It is the pie that has fish heads and tails poking through the pastry.

Locally 23 December is known as Tom Bawcock's Eve. Two hundred years ago, a severe storm prevented Mousehole fishermen from putting to sea and as it raged for weeks the village became desperate for their usual harvest of fish to eat and to sell.

Eventually Tom Bawcock dared all and put to sea with his nets in spite of dire warnings from the villagers. As his boat mounted the billows, suddenly the raging seas were calmed. It is a story with an almost biblical meaning, for shoals of fish then came to the surface. Tom secured a massive catch and his nets contained seven kinds of fish.

Generous Tom gave the fish to the hungry villagers who made Star Gazey Pies with the catch. To celebrate the event, the following song is sung in Cornish inns and firework displays take place.

A merry place you may believe
Was Mouzel on Tom Bawcock's Eve.
To be there then, who would not wish
To sup on seven sorts of fish?

NEWLYN

Newlyn is Cornwall's principal fishing port and years ago the local fishwives were renowned for their blue eyes and fresh complexions. They sold their husbands' catches of fish (mainly pilchards) in nearby Penzance. The Newlyn wives certainly stood out from the crowd in their scarlet coats and big, black beaver hats. 'Cowals' or baskets where their fish was kept were strapped to their foreheads.

Although Cornish pasties are as much in evidence in Newlyn as everywhere else in Cornwall, there were plenty of different ways of preparing fish. Every Bank Holiday Monday the Newlyn Fish Festival takes place. Stalls and cafés take over the quays for the day. The recipes I was told were old and tried.

Newlyn 100 years ago, when it was one of the busiest fishing ports in Cornwall.

Tomato Relish

Ingredients

3lb (1.35kg) tomatoes, skinned and chopped
½ pint (275ml) malt vinegar
1lb (450g) onions, peeled and chopped
8oz (225g) brown sugar
1 teaspoon finely ground sea salt

Method

- Place all the ingredients in a pan.
- Heat gently at first, then simmer steadily for around 1½ hours until mixture thickens.
- Pot.

Apple Chutney

Ingredients

1lb (450g) Bramley apples
1lb (450g) brown sugar
8oz (225g) seedless raisins
1 onion
1 teaspoon sea salt
¼ teaspoon nutmeg
¼ teaspoon allspice
1 pint (570ml) malt vinegar

Method

- Peel, core and chop apples. Peel and chop onion.
- Place together with the rest of the ingredients in a stainless steel pan.
- Let the sugar dissolve slowly then cook on until mushy, about 1½ hours, by which time the chutney will have thickened and be ready for potting.

Apple and Sultana Chutney

Ingredients

1½ pint (845mls) malt vinegar
1½lb (700g) brown sugar
1lb (450g) washed sultanas
2lb (900g) Bramley apples, peeled and cored
Muslin
1oz (25g) bruised root ginger
1oz (25g) pickling spice

Method

- Place the vinegar in a stainless steel pan.
- Add the brown sugar, sultanas and apples.
- Prepare a muslin bag containing the root ginger and pickling spice and add.
- Boil all ingredients over a low heat for almost 2 hours.
- Remove the muslin bag and discard.
- Pot the chutney in heated jars and cover securely.

Scalloped Potatoes

Method

- Mix flour, salt and baking powder.
- Slowly add sufficient cold water to form a coating consistency, being careful not to 'drown the miller'.
- Coat the potatoes in the batter and fry until golden brown.

Ingredients

1 tablespoon plain flour
1 level teaspoon baking powder
½ teaspoon cooking salt
3 large baking potatoes, peeled and sliced ¼in thick

Curried Fish Pies

Method

- Prepare as for flaky pastry.
- Leave for 20 minutes before using.
- Roll out thinly and cut into squares or circles.
- Chop the onion and sauté in pan containing the melted butter.
- Add the finely chopped apple.
- Stir in curry powder, flour, chutney, sultanas, lemon juice and salt.
- Add ¼ pint (150ml) water and simmer for 10 minutes.
- Add the flaked fish and chopped hard-boiled egg.
- Place the filling in spoonfuls in the middle of the pieces of pastry.
- Damp the edges of the pastry and seal in with a pastry top.
- Bake at 220°C/gas mark 7 oven for 20 minutes.

Ingredients

PASTRY

8oz (225g) plain flour sieved with 1 level teaspoon salt
6oz (175g) margarine
6 tablespoons water
1 teaspoon lemon juice

FILLING

1 small onion
1oz (25g) butter
½ cooking apple
1 teaspoon curry powder
1 teaspoon flour
1 teaspoon mango chutney
½ teaspoon lemon juice
½oz sultanas
4oz (110g) cooked haddock
1 hard-boiled egg
½ teaspoon sea salt

Cornish Easter Cake

Method

- Sieve the flour and salt into a basin and make a hollow in the centre.
- Beat the yeast and a teaspoon of caster sugar to a cream in another basin and add the lukewarm water. Pour into the hollow in the flour.
- Work in the flour gradually to a smooth dough.
- Cover and leave for one hour in a warm place to rise.
- Beat the butter and sugar to a cream and add the eggs one by one, beating well.
- When the dough has risen add the creamed butter and eggs, working in well until smooth.
- Stir in the fruit, spice and peel.
- Leave to rise again for another hour in a warm place.
- Put the mixture in a greased tin lined with two thicknesses of greased paper.
- Place the tin on a baking sheet and bake the cake for 2 hours at 160°C/gas mark 3. When cold, cover the cake all over with almond paste.
- Put a roll of paste round the top and bake at 160°C/gas mark 3 for 10 minutes to brown the almond paste very lightly.

Ingredients

8oz (225g) flour
½oz (10g) yeast
1 teaspoon caster sugar
1 gill (¼ pint) lukewarm water
8oz (225g) currants
4oz (110g) raisins
4oz (110g) candied peel shredded
1 teaspoon mixed spice
2 eggs
4oz (110g) butter
2oz (50g) sugar
1 teaspoon salt

Fish Flan

Method

- Line an 8in flan case with shortcrust pastry and bake.
- Poach the fish in a little milk.
- Make the white sauce with the milk from the fish, seasoning with the cayenne pepper and salt.
- As the sauce thickens add grated cheese and egg yolk.
- Fill the flan case with the flaked fish and cover with the sauce.
- Bake at 160°C/gas mark 3 for about 15 minutes.

Ingredients

12oz (350g) smoked haddock
½ pint (275ml) white cornflour sauce
1oz (25g) grated cheese
1 egg yolk
Salt and cayenne pepper

Some of the ingredients for batter. (Photograph courtesy Ron and Barbara Strachan)

Fritter Batter

Countywide amongst fruit fritters, apples seem to be the most popular but peaches and rhubarb were also made into fritters.

Ingredients

10oz (275g) flour
2 eggs
2oz (50g) butter
¼ pint (150ml) boiling water
½ pint (275ml) cold water

Method

- Pour the boiling water onto the butter then add a further ½ pint (275ml) of cold water.
- Mix in the flour until smooth.
- Stir in the whites of 2 eggs.

Ginger Honey Crunch Biscuits

Ingredients

8oz (225g) margarine
2 tablespoons runny honey
2oz (50g) crushed cornflakes
4oz (110g) caster sugar
10oz (275g) self-raising flour
2 teaspoons ginger

Method

- Cream the margarine and sugar.
- Add the other ingredients.
- Divide the mixture into small lumps.
- Place on a greased baking tray and flatten each lump with a fork.
- Bake at 160°C/gas mark 3 for 10–15 minutes.
- The recipe makes 36 biscuits.

Ginger honey crunch biscuits. (Photograph courtesy Elizabeth Hall)

Brown Bread Pudding

Method

- Mix together dry ingredients.
- Stir in the eggs and a little milk.
- Place in a greased bowl and cover with a cloth or greaseproof paper.
- Boil for 1½ hours.
- Melt the butter and pour in the sherry and rosewater.
- Stir in the sugar.
- Keep stirring for some time until a smooth sauce is obtained.
- Pour this over the brown bread pudding.

Ingredients

2oz (50g) flour
4oz (110g) brown breadcrumbs
8oz (225g) shredded suet
8oz (225g) currants
2oz (50g) caster sugar
4 eggs, beaten
A little milk
Grated nutmeg

FOR THE SAUCE

2oz (50g) butter
2 tablespoons sugar
2 tablespoons sherry
2 tablespoons rosewater

NEWQUAY

This popular Cornish resort has ten golden, sandy beaches, beloved of surfers, the most sheltered being Towan. The beaches are open to the Atlantic Ocean and bring international surfing champions to the town. For centuries it was a fishing village dependent on pilchards. Bronze Age barrows in the vicinity proclaim ancient origins, some from 4,000 years ago. In the nineteenth century, long rowing boats called gigs competed against each other, as they still do today, in a bay six miles off the coast of Truro and Devoran.

Fistral Bay, Newquay, *c.* 1933.

Towan beach, Newqay, *c.* 1933.

Savoury Pancakes

Method

- Gradually beat the 1 egg and the yolk only of a second egg into flour and salt.
- Add the milk slowly, beating well.
- Melt the butter and allow it to slip down side of dish into beaten mixture.
- Beat again very well.
- Allow to stand for ½ hour
- Sauté the chopped mushrooms in butter and add the chopped cold ham.
- Put in flour, stock and seasoning, stirring in the chopped eggs last.
- After whisking the batter which has been allowed to stand, make into pancakes, using butter in the frying pan.
- Keep warm in a dish, then to each one add the filling and cream.

Ingredients

FOR THE BATTER

4oz (110g) flour
½oz (10g) butter
1 egg
1 egg yolk
½ pint (275ml) milk
pinch of sea salt

FOR THE FILLING

4oz (110g) cold chopped ham or chicken and ham
2oz (50g) mushrooms
2oz (50g) butter
1oz (25g) flour
2 chopped, hard-boiled eggs
Seasoning to taste
1 tablespoon cream
¼ pint (150ml) stock
Grated cheese for garnish

Veal Loaf

Method

- Soak the breadcrumbs in the hot milk and squeeze out.
- Mince the veal and the unsoftened butter and add to the breadcrumbs with the grated lemon peel and seasoning.
- Beat the eggs and add to the mixture (save a little of the beaten eggs to brush over the loaf).
- Shape the veal loaf, brush with egg mixture and roll in the breadcrumbs.
- Place in a baking tin and bake at 220°C/gas mark 7 until nicely browned.
- After 20 minutes roll up the rashers of bacon and place on top of the loaf.
- When the bacon rolls have cooked, serve the veal loaf with slices of freshly cut, ripe tomatoes.

Ingredients

1oz (25g) butter, fresh from the fridge and chopped
8oz (225g) lightly cooked cold veal
2 eggs
1 cupful of fresh breadcrumbs
4 rashers of bacon
2 tablespoons of hot milk
The grated peel of 1 lemon
1 tablespoon dried breadcrumbs
Sea salt and pepper

Cheese Scotch Eggs

Method

- Whilst eggs are boiling, mash the potatoes well with the grated cheese.
- Flour the peeled hard-boiled eggs and cover with the mixture.
- Roll the eggs in beaten egg and breadcrumbs and deep fry in hot fat.

Ingredients

5 eggs
4oz (110g) grated cheese
1lb (450g) mashed potatoes
Seasoning to taste
Breadcrumbs for coating
Hot fat

Old Times Gingerbread

Called 'old times' in Newquay 1916, this recipe must also be well tried and tested.

Ingredients

1lb (450g) flour
2oz (50g) candied peel
6oz (175g) butter
1oz (25g) ground ginger
4oz (110g) sugar
1 teaspoon mixed spice
2oz (50g) almonds
½ teaspoon bicarbonate of soda
1 egg
8oz (225g) golden syrup

Method

- Chop the almonds and candied peel.
- Mix with the ginger, spice and flour.
- Slightly warm the syrup, butter and sugar, and beat to a cream.
- Add the egg.
- Dissolve the soda in a little warm milk and add.
- Bake in a slow oven for 2 hours, taking care not to shake or cool the gingerbread whilst in the oven.

Baking used to be done in the 'cloam' or bread oven. Furze faggots were set alight and allowed to flame out of the oven door so that the walls of the oven became very hot. Ashes were raked out, the 'bake' put in and door sealed, the loaves being left to cook before the oven cooled. The free-standing cloam oven remained unchanged from the sixteenth century and had a cross on the clay door to bless the bread.

Cornish Milk Bread

Ingredients

3lb (1.35kg) strong white flour
2 teaspoons salt
1 pint (570ml) tepid water
½ pint (275ml) tepid milk
1½oz (40g) yeast
2oz (50g) lard

Method

- Place flour and salt in a bowl and rub in the lard.
- Whisk the yeast into half the liquid and put into the bowl, mixing well.
- Add the remainder of the liquid and begin to knead the dough (the correct consistency is indicated when the sides of the mixing bowl are clean of all dough).
- Cover the dough with a damp tea towel and leave to almost double in size.
- Knead the dough again and shape into oblong loaves, placing these in well-greased warm tins.
- Bake at 220°C/gas mark 7 for 1 hour.

Meat Fuggan

Method

- Sieve the flour and the salt together and rub in the lard.
- Mix with water to a dry dough and form into the shape of a large, fat pasty.
- Make a slit down the centre, open it wide and put in the meat.
- Close the cut, nipping the sides together, and bake for 40 minutes at 220°C/gas mark 7.

Ingredients

1lb (450g) flour
4oz (110g) lard
6oz (175g) meat, finely cubed and seasoned
Salt

* Fuggan pastry is also used to make Somerset Oggy.

PADSTOW

In the sixth century, St Petroc sailed from Wales to Cornwall where he founded a monastery. It was later sacked by Viking invaders in AD 981. Local ship owners founded the Guild of St Petro; Sir Walter Raleigh used the Court House at Padstow when he was Warden of the Stannaries; emigrants bound for the New World sailed to Padstow but the entrance to the estuary, Doom Bar Sandbank was treacherous.

A local saying at Boscastle was:

From Padstow Bar to Lundy Light
Is a sailor's grave by day or night.

At Padstow we were given a recipe by Rick Stein, Head Chef at The Seafood Restaurant and much travelled television cook.

Pan-Fried Fillet of Monkfish with Garlic and Fennel

Ingredients *(serves 4)*

4oz (110g) semolina
4 tablespoons sunflower oil
16 large garlic cloves
2 tablespoons lemon juice
A splash of Pernod or Ricard
1lb (450g) fennel bulb, thinly sliced
Salt and freshly ground black pepper
1 pint (570ml) fish stock
½oz (10g) sprigs of fennel herb
4 x 8oz (225g) pieces prepared monkfish fillet

Method

- Put the semolina, 2 sliced cloves of garlic and all but 1 sprig of fennel into a food processor. Blend until the mixture resembles an aromatic pale-green powder.
- Cut the rest of the garlic cloves lengthways into long thin piece.

- Melt half the butter in a pan and add the garlic and sliced fennel. Fry over medium heat until lightly browned.
- Add the fish stock and some seasoning and simmer for 15 minutes until the fennel is tender.
- Pre-heat the oven to 200°C/gas mark 6.
- Coat the pieces of monkfish in the semolina mixture.
- Heat the oil in an ovenproof frying pan, add a small knob of butter and the monkfish pieces and fry over a moderate heat, turning now and then, until they are golden brown all over.
- Transfer the pan to the oven and cook the monkfish for a further 10 minutes.
- Remove the pan from the oven and lift the fillets onto a chopping board. Slice diagonally into thick slices, keeping each piece in shape.
- Transfer to a plate and keep warm.
- Add the sautéed fennel mixture, lemon juice, Pernod and remaining finely chopped fennel to the pan in which the monkfish was cooked.
- Simmer rapidly until slightly reduced, then add the remaining butter and simmer until it has blended in to make a rich sauce.
- Adjust the seasoning if necessary.
- Lift the fish on to 4 warmed plates and spoon some of the sauce around each piece.

Courtesy Rick Stein, Head Chef, The Seafood Restaurant, Padstow

When Sir Walter Raleigh was Warden of the Stannaries of Cornwall, he used the sixteenth-century courthouse at Padstow. Did he ever eat Hodge Podge, a medieval stew?

Mutton Hodge Podge

In July and August we found some very tall Babington's leeks. With their delicate garlic aroma, I wondered if they were tried out in other stews in Sir Walter Raleigh's day? The Cornish cloam oven was perfect for slow cooking.

Method

- Put the meat in the pan with the cold water and bring it to the boil.
- Add the vegetables, barley, seasoning and parsley.
- Reduce heat and simmer for 2 hours – long cooking brings out the flavour.

Ingredients

2lb (900g) neck of lamb
4oz (110g) peas
3oz (75g) peeled, chopped swede
1 tablespoon chopped parsley
4 pints (2.42 litres) water
1 small handful of soaked barley
Salt and pepper

PENZANCE

The recipes that follow were given to me by Mrs Horsfall, who spent her last years at the Penzance Abbey Hotel. She particularly liked the Pineapple Pavlova served there.

She had a great sense of humour and vivid memories of her days spent in Lancashire, when 'The Englishman' sailed outward bound from Fleetwood to Fowey carrying cheese and returned with china clay.

Nineteenth-century Penzance Harbour.

Pineapple Pavlova

Method

- Whip the egg whites in a perfectly clean, dry bowl, until stiff.
- Whip in the sugar ounce by ounce.
- Add the cornflour, lemon juice and vanilla essence.
- Put the mixture for meringue into a mould in an oiled baking tin and bake in a slow oven for 140°C/gas mark 1 for at least an hour.

Ingredients

3 egg whites
6oz (175g) caster sugar
1 teaspoon cornflour
1 teaspoon lemon juice
½ teaspoon vanilla essence
¼ pint (150ml) double cream
Pineapple slices
Cherries and angelica

- Allow to cool.
- Spoon on half the cream, cover with chopped pineapple slices.
- Add the rest of the cream and finish with the cherries and angelica.

This recipe came from *Domestic Cornish Cookery* (1831), which has between its leather-bound boards instructions on how to dress a turtle and to roast a sturgeon.

Potted Salmon

- Take a large piece of salmon, scale and wipe it, but do not wash.
- Salt very well and leave until the salt has melted and drained off.
- Season with crushed mace and a whole pepper.
- Lay it on bay leaves, cover with butter and cook in a close-lidded kettle.
- When well done, drain off the gravy and put into clean pots.
- When cold, the potted salmon should be covered with clarified butter.
- Any firm fish could be done in the same way.

POINT

Point and Penpol are usually spoken of together, two Cornish villages on Penpol and Restrongruet Creeks, both very peaceful and favoured for retirement but a century ago, tin and copper were mined. Pack horses carried the metals and pit props collected from boats.

Point Quay was originally known as Daniell's Point because the stone quay was built by a Mr Daniell. The inn on the village green (greens are a rarity in Cornwall) called the Bell was said to be haunted – it is now a private house.

Although the boatyard at Penpol has closed, traditionally designed rowing gigs are still made and proudly brought out at the Devoran Regatta.

Birthday Cake

The cake is based on Mrs Beeton's recipe from her book *Cookery and Household Management.* I think of this as a Cornish recipe because it has been eaten at so many birthdays in Cornwall. It was, of course, Queen Victoria's favourite sponge for her Raspberry Sandwich Cake. I always finish the top off with a simple lemon icing and decorate with candles, angelica and cherries but Mrs Beeton ladled on fresh fruit.

Point birthday cake. (Photograph courtesy Ron and Barbara Strachan)

Method

- Cream the fat and sugar thoroughly.
- Add the well-whisked eggs gradually, beating between each addition (add some flour if the mixture shows signs of curdling).
- Sift flour and baking powder and stir in lightly.
- Place mixture in a 7in sandwich tin and bake at 180°C/gas mark 4.

Ingredients

4oz (110g) butter
4oz (110g) caster sugar
4oz (110g) plain flour
2 eggs
1 level teaspoon baking powder

Raspberry Crumble

Method

- Rub the butter into the flour and place in the fridge whilst the raspberries are being picked over.
- Mix in the sugar, nuts and oats.
- Lay raspberries in an oven-proof dish. Scatter the crumble over the fruit and bake at 180°C/gas mark 4 for 30 minutes.

Ingredients

4oz (110g) flour
2oz (50g) sugar
1oz (25g) roasted nuts, chopped
2oz (50g) oats
3oz (75g) butter
1lb (450g) raspberries

Cornish 'clouted cream' (as it was called in the eighteenth century) is a must with this delicious sweet, but Cornish ice cream will do instead, especially on hot days.

Stella's Lemon Cheese

Spread on crusty bread or freshly baked scones. Can also be used as a filling for a sponge cake. The cheese should be used within one week.

Ingredients

3 small eggs, beaten
3 lemons, squeezed and the zest grated
3oz (75g) butter
6oz (175g) sugar
Pan of boiling water and an old crock or jug

Method

- Mix butter and sugar.
- Add eggs, lemon juice and rind.
- Using a wooden spoon, mix all ingredients together in a crock until thick. When the lemon cheese coats the back of the spoon, it is cooked.
- Cool and pour into jars.

Victoria sponge with Stella's lemon cheese. (Photograph courtesy Ron and Barbara Strachan)

POLMASSICK

Polmassick has become known for its vineyard and produces good English wine, just as the Romans, who planted in this sheltered, warm area enjoyed the grapes for wine making they so missed from living in Italy.

Elderberry Wine

Method

- Leave the raisins to marinate in the water for 7 days, then sieve.
- Boil the elderberry juice and add, when cold, to the raisin liquor.
- Add the yeast, on pieces of toast, and allow to work.
- Do not bung until all the working has done.
- Allow to stand in a warm place for a week, then bottle.
- The wine should keep for months if kept in a cool place.

Ingredients

10 pints (6 litres) water
5lb (2.25kg) seedless raisins, well chopped
1 teaspoon dried yeast
2 pints (1.21 litres) elderberry juice

POLPERRO

The Pol, a stream, runs through the village. The harbour dates back possibly to the thirteenth century. Narrow winding streets and a house set on props fascinate visitors as does the 'horse bus' into the village, which is pulled by a large Shire horse. Some of the old cottages where fishermen have lived for centuries still have the cloam ovens of old. Salting and pressing of pilchards was once the traditional industry and smuggling and knitting fishermen's pullovers kept the residents busy during dark, stormy winters.

In place of the traditional splits with jam and clotted cream, many farmhouses serve scones. Many of these scone recipes from Polperro were excellent, although we had white scones from Trengwainton and sultana scones at Killiow which equally lingered in the memory.

Quaint street in Polperro, *c.* 1953.

Scones

Method

- Sift the flour into a bowl and add the baking powder and salt.
- Beat the egg with the milk.
- Make a well in the centre of the flour mixture and pour in the egg and milk mixture, gradually drawing the flour from the sides into the liquid.
- Knead the dough on a floured board.
- Roll and cut into rounds, 3in across.
- Glaze the tops with beaten egg or milk.
- Bake at 200°C/gas mark 6 for 20 minutes.

Ingredients

3oz (75g) butter
1lb (450g) flour
1 large egg
2 teaspoons baking powder
A little tepid milk
¼ teaspoon salt

Summer Pudding

Method

- Grease a pudding basin and line with the bread slices.
- Pile the stewed fruit into the basin (a little sugar added to the fruit will make the pudding juicier).
- Cover the top with a lid of bread.
- Weight the pudding and serve the next day with Cornish Cream.

Ingredients

Slices of trimmed white bread, not too thick
Stewed red/blackcurrants, blackberries, raspberries or any juicy summer fruits

Rum Butter

Rum butter was a treat at harvest time as well as Christmas. All the family had helped with the harvest from the young to the elderly. In bygone days the harvest was the most important social and economic event of the year, for a good harvest was something to rejoice over. When the reapers had cut the last sheaf of corn it was the custom to raise it into the air and give the 'Harvest Shout':

Well ploughed, well sowed,
Well harrowed, well mowed.
And all carted to the barn
With a nary a load throwed
Hooray!

Traditionally the rum butter was placed in a basin and well covered. Some of the special rum-butter basins were beautifully decorated and kept in the family as an heirloom.

Method

- Beat the butter over a gentle heat until it is soft and creamy, but do not let it turn to oil.
- Mix the spices with the sugar and beat into the butter.
- Add the rum, still beating.
- Place in a basin.

Ingredients

8oz (225g) soft brown sugar
4oz (110g) unsalted butter
2 tablespoons of rum
½ teaspoon of nutmeg
¼ teaspoon of cinnamon

POLZEATH

Polzeath has perfect conditions for surfers. Both Polzeath and New Polzeath overlook the wide sands of Hayle Bay. Looking across the Camel Estuary, the lofty headland of Stepper Point is unmissable. Paths to Rumps Point cross over an Iron Age fort.

The Georgian mansion, Pencarrow House, is within reach and open in summer.

Polzeath Beef Casserole

This Cornish recipe belongs to the days when, in the old kitchens, fires were kept burning all day. In farmhouses it was a tradition never to let the fire go out. Slow-burning peat was used throughout the night to keep the fire alive. Faggots of furze and wood kindling were kept in the ookner, a part of the range.

Method

- Put all ingredients into a casserole dish.
- Cook at 190°C/gas mark 5 for 2 hours.

Ingredients

1½lb (700g) cubed stewing steak
8oz (225g) carrots, sliced
8oz (225g) onions. sliced
¾ pint cold water
Seasoning to taste
A bunch of fresh herbs

Rolled Beef

A recipe from the ladies of the Women's Institute.

Ingredients

1½lb (700g) braising steak
4oz (110g) fine, dry breadcrumbs
2oz (50g) grated suet
1 egg
½ teaspoon parsley
½ teaspoon sage
½ pint of stock
Salt and pepper
1oz (25g) flour

Method

- ❖ Bind the suet, seasoning, breadcrumbs, parsley and sage with the egg and spread over the beef.
- ❖ Roll up and tie with string.
- ❖ Place in a deep pie dish with the stock.
- ❖ Cover and cook slowly for 2 hours.
- ❖ Remove the meat and thicken remaining liquid with flour.

ST CLEMENTS

St Clement's Church lies near the River Tresillian and dates to the thirteenth century. In the churchyard is a National Monument, an ignioc stone which formerly stood in the Old Vicarage drive opposite the creek. In the church porch are the former village stocks.

The manor of Morensk was one of the most important in Cornwall.

Fudge

Ingredients

2lb (900g) granulated sugar
¾ pint (426ml) milk
4oz (110g) butter, cut into small pieces
Few drops vanilla essence

Method

- ❖ Place the sugar in a large pan.
- ❖ Add the milk and dissolve the sugar slowly.
- ❖ Bring to the boil, until when tested, a small quantity dropped into cold water holds together.
- ❖ Add the butter and the vanilla essence.
- ❖ Beat with a wooden spoon until the fudge thickens, then pour immediately into a tin.

(To achieve a thicker fudge use Cornish cream.)

Bills Yates' Treacle Dunkers

The late Bill Yates was a good friend of ours and a super cook.

Ingredients

4oz (110g) butter
5oz (150g) brown sugar
2 good tablespoons black treacle
4oz (110g) flour
3oz (75g) rolled oats
1oz (25g) coconut
1 good teaspoon bicarbonate of soda, dissolved in 1 tablespoon of milk

Method

- In a pan slowly melt together the butter, sugar and treacle.
- In a bowl mix together the flour, coconut and rolled oats.
- Add the bicarbonate of soda and milk mixture.
- Losing no time, keep stirring, blending in the mixture from the pan.
- Bake on a metal sheet at 160°C/gas mark 3 for 25 minutes. When cool, cut into fingers.

Bill's treacle dunkers. (Photograph courtesy Ron and Barbara Strachan)

Bill Yates' Coconut Cake

Ingredients

8oz (225g) butter
8oz (225g) sugar
2 eggs, beaten
4oz (110g) sifted self-raising flour
4oz (110g) coarse coconut

Method

- Cream together butter and sugar.
- Beat in the 2 eggs.
- Sift in the flour and coconut.
- Place in a tin lined with baking parchment/greaseproof paper, and bake at the top of the oven heated to 160°C/gas mark 3 for 35 minutes.

ST IVES

The town is named after St Ia who was a saint who sailed from Ireland to the Cornish shore in a coracle. The maze of narrow streets is paved with granite and nestle between the harbour and Porthmeor Beach. The town attracts artists; the beach attracts surfers.

Smeaton, the engineer who pioneered the building of the Eddystone Lighthouse in 1759, also designed St Ives Harbour, helping the town to become Cornwall's foremost pilchard port in the nineteenth century.

Smeaton's stone pier in St Ives, built in 1770, is shown in this postcard, *c.* 1933.

The Sloop Inn, St Ives, *c.* 1928.

Fig Pudding

Method

- Finely cut up the figs and grate the suet.
- Add the eggs and a little grated nutmeg.
- Stir in the sugar and breadcrumbs until well mixed.
- Boil all ingredients together in a well-buttered basin for 4 hours, topping up the water as required.

Ingredients

8oz (225g) breadcrumbs
8oz (225g) fresh figs
6oz (175g) sugar
6oz (175g) suet
2 eggs, beaten
Grated nutmeg

Prince Albert's Pudding

Ingredients

4oz (110g) sugar
4oz (110g) flour
4oz (110g) chopped raisins
3 eggs, beaten
Grated rind 1 lemon
2oz (50g) butter

Method

- ❖ Cream the butter and sugar together.
- ❖ Add the remaining ingredients, the raisins last.
- ❖ Boil in a well-buttered basin for 3 hours.

Golden Plum Charlotte

Ingredients

Slices of bread and butter
Brown sugar
1lb (450g) golden plums
2oz (50g) sugar

Method

- ❖ Butter a shallow pie dish and line with the slices of bread and butter.
- ❖ Halve the plums and pack into dish, cut side up, adding sugar to the layers.
- ❖ Cover with bread and butter, butter side uppermost.
- ❖ Bake in a medium-heated oven until plums are cooked, about 35 minutes.
- ❖ Turn out of dish and serve with clotted cream.

Brown Betty

Ingredients

1lb (450g) cooking apples, washed, peeled, cored and sliced very thinly
4oz (110g) brown breadcrumbs
2oz (50g) Demerara sugar
Grated rind and juice of 1 lemon
3 tablespoons syrup
1 teaspoon allspice

Method

- ❖ Place a layer of apples in a pie dish. Cover with the breadcrumbs and sprinkle with the sugar and spices.
- ❖ Repeat these layers.
- ❖ When the dish is full, add the lemon juice and syrup and scatter the lemon rind over the top.
- ❖ Bake at 160°C/gas mark 3 for 30 minutes.
- ❖ Serve with Cornish cream.

St Just in Roseland

Lying on the Roseland Peninsula, this beautiful village boasts a church with an unusual thirteenth-century castellated tower, and the villagers declare that their church is 'the most beautiful in the land'.

The area is warm and sheltered and bamboos grow to 20ft high. Other plants that thrive in this atmosphere include palms, azaleas, magnolias, a strawberry tree, a Chilean pine and fountains of golden broom.

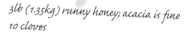

The grey stone church in St Just in Roseland.

Lemon Mead

Ingredients

3lb (1.35kg) runny honey; acacia is fine
10 cloves
2 sprigs rosemary
1 teaspoon yeast
6 lemons
1 piece of root ginger, sliced
8 pints (4.5 litres) water
1lb (450g) sugar

Method

- Boil the water, honey and sugar together for 15 minutes.
- Add the cloves, ginger and rosemary.
- Cut the lemons in half and place flat at the base of a large, earthenware bowl.
- Pour over the boiling liquor.
- Spread two pieces of toast with the yeast and leave to work with the mead. Skim and remove the toast when they have done working.
- Leave for a week and then bottle.

St Michael's Mount

St Michael's Mount and causeway, *c.* 1950.

Cornish Splits

This recipe was kindly given to me by Jayne Spenceley at the Sail Loft Restaurant at St Michael's Mount in the 1960s. The Cornish splits made there were gorgeous, split open and crammed with Cornish cream and homemade strawberry jam.

The Sail Loft Restaurant is said by the National Trust to be an 'exemplar restaurant' which sources and uses good-quality local food.

Method

- Rub the margarine into the flour and salt mixture using the finger tips.
- Crumble the yeast liquid on to the flour and add the remainder of the tepid milk, drawing the dough together with the hands.
- Turn the dough onto a lightly floured board, kneading it well for 10 minutes to work the yeast throughout. The best dough is firm and stretchy but not sticky.
- Cover the dough with a large, upturned mixing bowl or polythene. Leave for 10 minutes.

Ingredients

3lb (1.35kg) plain, strong white flour
1½oz (40g) sugar
1½oz (40g) yeast
1½oz (40g) margarine
Pinch of salt
1 pint (570ml) milk

- Preheat the oven to 230°C/gas mark 8.
- Keep everything warm and divide the risen dough into portions to make the splits, rolling each into a ball.
- Place on large, greased trays for 20 minutes to double in size.
- Bake at the top of the oven for 20 minutes.

SENNEN COVE

The village is remote from any habitation and is England's most westerly mainland village. The granite tower of the church dates from the fifteenth century, when the villagers sought permission to bury their dead around the ancient chapel as it was so dangerous to take corpses for burial at St Burgan. Their fear was of sudden raids upon their village by pirates.

Legend has it that King Arthur marched from Tintagel to Sennen to defeat the invading Danes, and having won the battle, he and his knights feasted at the huge, granite Tablemen Stone.

Sennen Cove is connected in my mind with Praa Sands, white and silvery (but dangerous for bathing). We came away without a recipe, but one arrived in the post with instructions that both Heavy Cake and Saffron Cake must appear – no Cornish cookery book could do without them.

Sennen Heavy Cake

Method

- Rub the margarine into the flour and add all the other ingredients except the candied peel and 4oz (110g) of the butter.
- Mix well and make into a dough by adding the milk.
- Roll into a strip and dot with 2oz (50g) of the butter.
- Fold in three, roll out and dot with the remaining 2oz (50g) of the butter.
- Repeat just the folding and rolling out once more.
- Roll out to 1in thick and divide into 4 pieces, marking the tops of each with a diamond pattern.
- Brush with milk and bake at 200°C/gas mark 6 for 25 minutes. Decorate with the candied peel.

Ingredients

1 pint (570ml) milk
1 teaspoon baking powder
6oz (175g) sugar
8oz (225g) margarine
2lb (900g) plain flour
½ teaspoon slat
1lb (450g) currants
8oz (225g) butter
Candied peel (see recipe overleaf)
Milk for glazing

Candied Peel

A second boiling in cold, fresh water, before the simmering in sugar syrup improves the taste of the peel even more.

Method

- Slice the peel with its pith removed and cover with water.
- Simmer gently until the peel assumes a translucent appearance.
- Simmer for a further 10 minutes in a teacup full of sugar dissolved in ½ teacup of water.
- Roll out the pieces of peel in the caster sugar.
- Pack the candied peel into airtight jars.

Ingredients

Orange, grapefruit and lemon peel
Teacup of sugar
Caster sugar

TINTAGEL

The old Post Office at Tintagel is the most interesting building left in this romantically sited village. Built of Cornish brown slate this fourteenth-century manor house was saved by Miss Catherine Johns.

The Victorian poets, Tennyson, Arnold and Swinburne believed that Tintagel was King Arthur's legendary birthplace and thus its popularity led to the destruction of old cottages and vernacular architecture.

In 1900, the National Trust bought this rare survival for £100.

Many old recipes are simple and basic, yet the method of preparation ensures a tastiness which continues to please. The following recipes came from school cook, Mrs Bateson, and were popular with the children at the village school in the days of 'school dinners'. On her retirement she promised to collect and print her recipes. Here are three with considerably reduced quantities, serving only 3-4 people.

The old Post Office at Tintagel. This fourteenth-century small manor house was saved for posterity by Miss Catherine Johns.

Beef Soup

Method

- Cut the beef into small portions.
- Add 8 pints (4½ litres) water and rice, bring slowly to the boil.
- Add the chopped vegetables, plus one teaspoon of salt and a dash of pepper.
- Simmer slowly until all the ingredients are tender.
- Liquidise in a blender; serve with a blob of cream in each portion, centrally placed.

Ingredients

4oz (110g) lean beef
4oz (110g) rice
1 small turnip
1 carrot
1 tomato
3 stalks of celery
3 sprigs of parsley

Chocolate Cake

Method

- Cream the butter with the sugar.
- Beat in the eggs and milk, then add the cocoa and sifted flour until all is mixed well together.
- Divide the mixture between two 8in sandwich tins and bake at 180°C/gas mark 4 for 30 minutes.
- Remove from tins when cold.
- Sandwich the two portions together with melted chocolate or Cornish cream.

Ingredients

8oz (225g) butter
8oz (225g) soft brown sugar
2oz (50g) cocoa
6oz (175g) self-raising flour
4 eggs
4 tablespoons milk

Orange Sauce

Method

- Mix the sugar and cornflour to a smooth cream with a little of the water.
- Boil the rest of the water and add the creamed cornflour slowly.
- Cook until the mixture thickens, putting in the orange rind and juice last of all to retain the flavour. Then scatter the nutmeg and drop the ounce of butter into the sauce.

Ingredients

1 tablespoon cornflour
½ pint water
4 tablespoons finely pounded sugar
1oz (25g) butter
Grated rind and juice of 1 orange
Pinch of nutmeg

(Lemon sauce can be made in the same way by sub-stituting lemon rind and juice.)

TRELISSICK

This beautiful landscaped garden and woodland by the River Fal was, in the nineteenth century, owned by 'guinea-a-minute Gilbert'. This wealthy man could gallop to Truro and all the land he covered on his horseback journey was owned by himself, his fortune coming from tin and copper mines on his estate. The National Trust administer the beautiful gardens of Trelissick, Trerice and Lanhydrock and offer a high standard of catering, the perfect complement to a day spent wandering in superb grounds at any season of the year.

This is not a National Trust recipe but given to me by a Cornish friend. The soup is so redolent of Trelissick, for which we have so many happy memories. On the woodland walk we saw squirrels, herons, curlew and cheeky robins which sat down with us, whenever we did. This soup is made from fresh tomatoes, ripe and red – 'love apples' as they were known in Cornwall.

The Water Tower at Trelissick Gardens, 1998.

Celtic cross at Trelissick.

Tomato Soup

Ingredients

1½lb (700g) tomatoes, skinned by pouring boiling water over them, then peel as the skins split
1oz (25g) butter
1½ pints (845ml) chicken stock
½ teaspoon black pepper
2 teaspoons sugar
Thinly pared rind of 1 orange
1 onion, well chopped
1 bay leaf
Freshly ground sea salt
3 teaspoons lemon juice
Rosemary sprigs, chopped parsley and cream to garnish

Method

- Melt the butter in saucepan over low heat.
- Add the quartered, skinned tomatoes and cook for 10 minutes, stirring well.
- Gradually add the stock, onion, bay leaf, orange rind and seasoning.
- When the liquid boils, turn the heat to low, cover the pan and simmer for 40 minutes.
- The contents can then be blended in a liquidiser.
- Reheat the soup, adding the lemon juice.
- Individual bowls of the soup may look tempting if decorated with a sprig of rosemary and a teaspoon of chopped parsley in the centre, surrounded by a swirl of cream.

TRELISKE

Marmalade Turnovers

Ingredients

2 eggs
Weight of one egg in both butter and flour
½ pint (275ml) milk
Marmalade
1 dessertspoon caster sugar

Method

- Cream butter and sugar together.
- Add flour, milk and eggs and mix well.
- Pour batter into greased saucers.
- Bake in a moderate oven 160°C/gas mark 3 for about 15-20 minutes, but do not let turnovers harden.
- Put in marmalade and turn over like turnovers.
- Sift white sugar over, and serve hot.

Parkin

Method

- Rub the lard and margarine into the dry ingredients.
- Melt sugar and syrup together and mix into the dry ingredients.
- Moisten with 5oz (140g) milk. Stir well.
- Bake in a medium oven for 45 minutes to an hour.

Ingredients

8oz (225g) oatmeal
8oz (225g) flour
3oz (75g) lard
3oz (75g) margarine
6 tablespoons syrup
5oz (150g) brown sugar
1 dessertspoon ginger
1 teaspoon baking powder

TRELOWARREN

From Trelowarren House we tramped the long walk through the spacious grounds and never met a soul. It was unchanged over years and parts were apparently untended. We found ourselves having to crawl under felled giants of trees, left after the great storm that swept the south of England in 1987.

We passed a cottage with an enormous piece of its thatched roof missing. Half an hour later we found it in a field. It was too far to go back and tell the cottager who had related the events of the fierce night's storm, but we did leave word at the small café close to Trelowarren House.

The cottage at Trelowarren which lost part of its thatch in the great storm of 1987.

Salmon and Cucumber Cups

Method

- ❖ Line patty tins with the pastry and bake blind at 220°C/gas mark 7.
- ❖ Dice half of the cucumber, salmon and salad cream and place the mixture in the pastry cases.
- ❖ Decorate with the remainder of the cucumber, sliced very thinly.

Ingredients

6oz (175g) shortcrust pastry
1 small tin salmon
½ cucumber, diced
3 tablespoons of salad cream

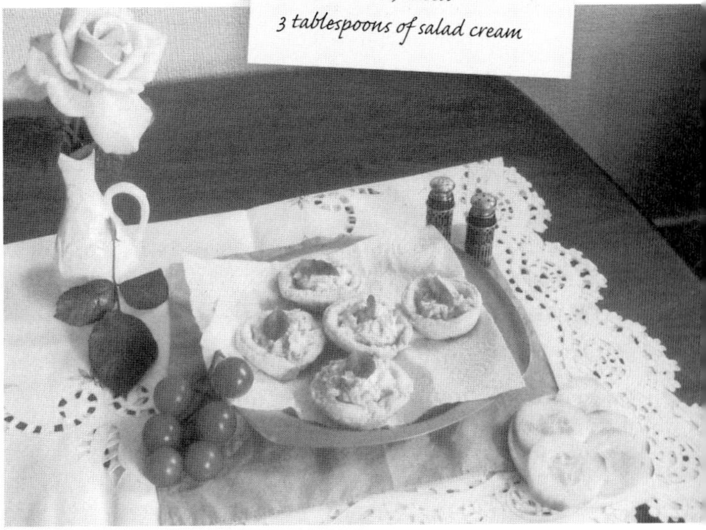

Salmon and cucumber cups. (Photograph courtesy Ron and Barbara Strachan)

TRERICE

Children from St Newlyn East Primary School worked with the National Trust to create an award-winning vegetable and herb Tudor garden. The produce is used to make delicious food in the restaurant at Trerice Gardens.

The favourite sweet in the garden's restaurant is lemon meringue pie, known in the Tudor period as 'transparent tart'.

Trerice Manor near Newquay.

Lemon Meringue Pie

Ingredients

8oz pastry
2 tablespoons cornflour
2oz (50g) sugar
Grated rind and juice of 2 lemons
¼ pint (150ml) water
2 egg yolks (and 2 egg whites for the meringue)
½oz (10g) butter

Method

- Prepare the pastry and line an 8in flan tin. Prick well all over. Line with foil to keep pastry flat and bake at 200°C/gas mark 6 for 15 minutes. Remove foil and return to oven for a further 15 minutes.
- For the filling, place the cornflour, sugar and lemon rind into a basin and mix to a smooth paste with water.
- Heat the rest of the water and lemon juice and work into the paste.
- Put into a pan and stir until the mixture thickens. Simmer for 2½ minutes.
- Beat in the egg yolks and the butter. Gently cook for a further minute and then pour carefully into the flan case (slowly and without shaking).
- Bake in a moderate oven at 180°C/gas mark 4.
- Allow to cool.

Meringue Topping

Ingredients

2oz (50g) of whites of eggs
To every egg white allow 2oz (50g) caster sugar
A little icing sugar for dredging
A forcing bag
A greased baking sheet or tin if separate meringues are wanted

THERE ARE CERTAIN RULES TO ENSURE SUCCESS

! The eggs must be very fresh.
! The whites must be carefully divided from the yolks as no yolk must mix with whites.
! Use a whisk to beat the whites.
! Make sure that both dish and whisk are perfectly clean.

Method

- Tap each egg smartly on the edge of the dish to gently crack shell, holding the egg upright over the dish.
- Lift off the top half of the eggshell and allow the white to drop into the basin. Hold steady and the yolk will stay put.
- Whisk the whites until they are stiff and dry then fold in the caster sugar.
- Gently drop the mixture into a forcing bag.
- Turn back the top of the bag, then press the mixture on to the prepared tin, if you desire individual shapes, or pipe it on to the pie top.
- Place in a cool oven at 120°C/gas mark ½ until the meringue becomes set and firm.

Whereas a few drops of flavouring essence can be added to the mixture, never use fruit juice. In the case of lemon meringue pie, no flavouring should be used.

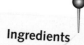

TREVARNO

Walter de la Mare asked, 'who said peacock pie?' in one of his poems. Peacock pie was doubtless served up at Pendennis and St Mawes castles long ago; indeed whole cooked peacocks were brought to the groaning table in the great hall, dressed with their feathers. Today we must be content with a peacock displaying to his peahens outside the restaurant at Trevarno House. There will be a recipe somewhere but thankfully I did not find it in Cornwall. The following recipe is much more homely.

Peacocks and peahens outside the restaurant at Trevarno near Helston.

An old pump in the woods at Trevarno.

Steak and Onions

Ingredients

4 portions of rump steak
2lb (900g) onions, peeled and thinly sliced
1oz (35g) butter
Sea salt

Method

- Place onions in a pan of boiling water with ½ teaspoon salt. After 20 minutes of boiling, strain and place a in a frying pan with the butter. Cook gently, stirring frequently.
- Brush the 4 portions of steak with butter and place under a red-hot grill to brown. Do not pierce the portions with a fork when turning to brown the other sides.
- Initially cook quickly to seal in the meat juices, then grill slowly to make steak tender, turning 3 times and taking around 20 minutes, according to thickness of steak.
- Meanwhile, the onions should be kept hot and as soon as the steak is ready, pile them around the meat.

(The Victorians ate this accompanied with Lea & Perrins Worcestershire Sauce.)

TRENGWAINTON

A great variety of fruit, vegetable and cut flowers will be grown (it is hoped) in the garden at Trengwainton, even olives and citrus fruits, for Cornwall's climate is particularly mild here.

The walled garden was built in 1826 by Sir Rose Price. At that time, England was suffering from unusually cold temperatures. Sloping beds, a good geographical position and increased drainage helped food production and the garden became nationally important, an historical asset to England.

Below is a recipe as old as the ancient Greeks who enjoyed this delicious sweet, soon to be revived at the National Trust garden of Trengwainton. Greek yoghurt goes well with these juicy figs, but they are good enough without any dressing.

Figs with Chopped Almonds

Cut as many fresh figs as you wish to use in half and gently flatten them. They must then be dried in the sun or in a low oven if sun not showing. The outside must be dry but the inside of the figs should remain still sticky.

Sprinkle half of each fig with toasted, chopped almonds and press the two halves together.

TREWITHEN

Trewithen is an eighteenth-century estate which has been in the same family for ten generations. It was mentioned in the Domesday Book but today has a tearoom where homemade cakes are welcomed. There is also a small museum and an interesting Camera Obscura Crane. Amidst twenty-four 'Champion Trees', famed for their height and viewing platform, is a renowned collection of camellias and magnolias.

Carrot and Apple Salad

Ingredients

4 tablespoons grated raw carrot
1 tablespoon seedless raisins
1 tablespoon thin cream
4 tablespoons chopped apple
2 teaspoons lemon juice
Crisp watercress and lettuce for a base

Method

- Pour the lemon juice and the cream in a bowl.
- Blend in the carrot, raisin and apple.
- Pile on to the green base.

Mushroom and Tomato Flan

Method

- Rub the fat into the flour. Add the salt and water to form shortcrust pastry.
- Wash and cut up the mushrooms and sauté in a little butter.
- Add the milk to the beaten eggs. Season and beat well.
- Line a flan case with the pastry.
- Put in the mushrooms and pour over the egg and milk mixture.
- Add thin slices of tomato to decorate and bake for 40 minutes at 190°C/gas mark 5.

Ingredients

8oz (225g) plain flour
4oz (110g) margarine
Cold water and a pinch of salt
4oz (110g) mushrooms
4oz (110g) tomatoes
½ pint milk (275ml) milk
1oz (25g) butter
2 eggs, beaten
Seasoning

Asparagus Pâté

Method

- Liquidise all the ingredients except the cucumber.
- Add the cucumber.
- Pour into a wetted mould to set, and then refrigerate.
- When turned out the pâté can be decorated with more cucumber, thinly sliced.

Ingredients

10oz (275g) fresh asparagus
3oz (75g) melted butter
3oz (75g) cheese
1 tablespoon lemon juice
½oz (15g) gelatine, dissolved in a little water
1in (2.5cm) cucumber, chopped
Freshly ground salt and black peppercorns

Artichoke Mousse with Tomato Sauce

Method for the Artichoke Mousse

- Mix the artichoke purée, cream and eggs (whole and yolks).
- Strain through a fine sieve and season to taste. Butter four 4in ramekins and fill with the mixture.
- Cover with tinfoil and cook in a bain-marie at 200°C/gas mark 6 for 30-35 minutes, or until mixture is set to the touch.

Ingredients

¼ pint (150ml) Jerusalem artichoke purée
½ pint double cream
1 egg
3 egg yolks
Salt and ground white pepper
Small leaves of parsley or chervil for garnish

For the Tomato Sauce

- Place all ingredients in a pan and boil for 5 minutes.
- Liquidise, strain and season.

To finish:

Unmould mousses onto plates. Pour hot sauce around each one and decorate with a small leaf of parsley or chervil.

Ingredients

8 soft tomatoes
1 dessertspoon tomato purée
6oz (175g) double cream
2 shallots or small onions, chopped
2oz (50ml) water

TRURO

It is strange to think that a cathedral town as smart, clean and comely as Truro exported tin in the Middle Ages. Being one of four stannary towns in Cornwall, the city had the right to weigh and place a tax on tin until the nineteenth century.

A stone in the old city hall (originally the market hall) and dated 1615 is inscribed with a warning to dishonest traders:

Who seeks to find eternal treasure
Must use no guile in weight or measure.

Jack Phillimore's Seedy Cake

Jack Phillimore was one of a team of Cornish workmen at Pendennis Castle. The team discussed favourite Cornish food with me, for example, the aforementioned Star Gazey Pie. This was almost 20 years ago.

Method

- Cream the butter and sugar together.
- Add eggs, one at a time, beating well.
- Sift in the flour, baking powder and caraway seeds.
- Add the milk gradually until a dropping consistency is achieved.
- Line an 8in tin with greaseproof paper and bake at 180°C/gas mark 4.
- The centre of the cake should be tested with a thin skewer to see if the mixture inside emerges as cooked, rather than sticky. Usually the timing is about 1 hour.

Ingredients

4oz (110g) butter
4oz (110g) flour
½ teaspoon baking powder
4oz (110g) sugar
2 eggs
¼ pint (150ml) milk
1 heaped teaspoon of caraway seeds

Rose water

Gather one pint of fragrant, scented rose petals on a still, dry day. Place them in a basin and cover with one pint of boiling water that has been filtered first. Leave it to infuse for at least an hour. Strain through a sieve and pour into bottles. Cork lightly and use as a tonic to splash on body or face.

Pot Pourri

Gather and dry a quantity of fragrantly scented rose petals. Mix one dessertspoon of powdered borax with the same of salt and one teaspoon of powdered cinnamon. The mixture should then be added to two quarts of dried rose petals and stirred well.

The fragrance of pot pourri is released when the bowls are left in warm sunshine, in porches or on window ledges facing south.

Pot pourri. (Photograph courtesy Ron and Barbara Strachan)

A 'Delicious Dish of Apples' (1860 recipe)

Ingredients

8oz (225g) sugar
1 pint (570ml) water
2lb (900g) apples, pared and cored
The peel of two small lemons

Method

- Boil the sugar in the water for 20 minutes.
- Add the apples and lemon rind and boil until quite stiff.
- Put into two moulds and set in a cool place.
- When cold, turn out.
- Use fresh.
- Do not put in the fridge – for some reason cooked apples left in the fridge deteriorate in flavour.

A delicious dish of apples. (Photograph courtesy Ron and Barbara Strachan)

Truro Pork Pie

This is a hearty dish to enjoy with Cornish chutney or pickled walnuts. Unable to find a Cornish recipe for pickled walnuts, I include my father's.

Ingredients

2lb (900g) pork
3oz (75g) butter
3 dessert apples, peeled, cored and thinly sliced
2oz (50g) sugar
Pepper
Nutmeg
Glass white wine

Ingredients for pie crust

10oz (275g) plain flour
¼ pint (150ml) milk
4oz (110g) lard
Salt and pepper
1 beaten egg yolk to glaze

Method

- Unlike short pastry, this pastry should be kept warm.
- Sift the salt and pepper with the flour and in a warm bowl
- Heat the milk and lard together, add to the flour and mix well.
- Knead for 10 minutes when cool enough, and then cover with a warm, damp tea cloth.
- Roll out and mould pastry into a shape to receive the pork and apple.
- Cut the pork into strips and season well with the salt, pepper and nutmeg.
- Alternatively layer pork and apples inside the pastry.
- Pour in the wine, scatter on the sugar and dab on the butter in small pieces.
- Put on a pie-crust lid, dampening to secure it to the main pie and brushing over the lid with egg yolk.
- Bake at 160°C/gas mark 3.

Pickled Walnuts

Ingredients

Walnuts, picked when green, in early July
2 quarts (4 pints) water
4oz (110g) rock salt
Quantity of pickling spice in malt vinegar

Method

- Prick the walnuts all over.
- Make the brine solution, mixing the water with the rock salt.
- Soak the walnuts in the brine for one week.
- Drain the walnuts and allow to dry in the sun for three days. (Dad spread his on a cloth on the shed roof until they were black and shrivelled).
- Boil the walnuts, with enough pickling spice in malt vinegar to cover them, for 20 minutes.
- Pack in jars, cover with the vinegar liquid.

Pixie Cakes

I christened these delightful cakes myself after talking to the ladies who make them and serve welcome coffee in Truro Cathedral. After the apple harvest, which lasts until November, the smallest apples are left on the trees for the pixies, who, I feel sure, would equally enjoy these cakes in the unlikely event of there being any left.

Method

- Cream the butter and sugar.
- Mix in the beaten egg and milk, whisking well.
- Fold in the flour and add the currants.
- Bake in frilly paper cases on a baking sheet at 170°C/gas mark 3-4 for about 25 minutes until golden.

Ingredients

8oz (225g) plain flour
6oz (175g) butter or margarine
5oz (150g) sugar
1 large egg
1½oz washed currants
Milk to mix to a dropping consistency

Pixie cakes. (Photograph courtesy Ron and Barbara Strachan)

ZENNOR

The ancient, tiny village of Zennor is best viewed from Trewey Hill. It nestles under the granite mass of Zennor Hill and faces the Atlantic Ocean. Amidst this wild and romantic landscape in the centre of the village is the twelfth-century granite church of St Senara.

Our sightseeing group was told of an occasion when a lady from London remarked, 'How poor and mean are the surroundings'. She was answered by an indignant pensioner, 'Madam, Zennor was a church town when London was just a huddle of mud huts.'

The earliest record of a church at Zennor is 1150 but there was a Celtic church in existence from the sixth century.

The famous carved figure of the mermaid, possibly 700 years old, made me wonder if it inspired poet Matthew Arnold to write *The Forsaken Merman*. The story relates that a chorister from St Senara was lured into the sea by a mermaid holding a comb and mirror at what is known as Mermaid's Cove.

D.H. Lawrence wrote to Katherine Mansfield and Middleton Murry from Zennor in 1916, 'Lovelier than the Mediterranean, all gorse flickering with flowers and then the heather and foxgloves … it is the best place I have been in'.

Pilgrim's Cross outside St Senara's Church, Zennor.

Wholemeal Bread

Method

Ingredients

1½lb (700g) wholemeal flour
1oz (25g) fresh yeast
1oz margarine
1 beaten egg
1 teaspoon ground sea salt
¼ pint tepid water
A little oatmeal

- Mix the flour with the salt and rub in the margarine lightly, using the fingertips.
- Crumble the yeast into the warm water and stir.
- Pour the yeast liquid on to the flour and mix well with the hands to form dough.
- On a floured surface, knead the dough and cover with a tea cloth.
- Leave for 10 minutes and grease 2 loaf tins.
- Pre-heat the oven to 230°C/gas mark 8.
- Divide the dough into 2 portions shaped like the tins.
- Place in the tins and leave to prove (increase in size) for 35 minutes, covered with a damp tea cloth.
- Glaze the loaves with beaten egg and sprinkle oatmeal on top.
- Bake near the top of the oven for 40 minutes.
- When cool, turn out of the tins.

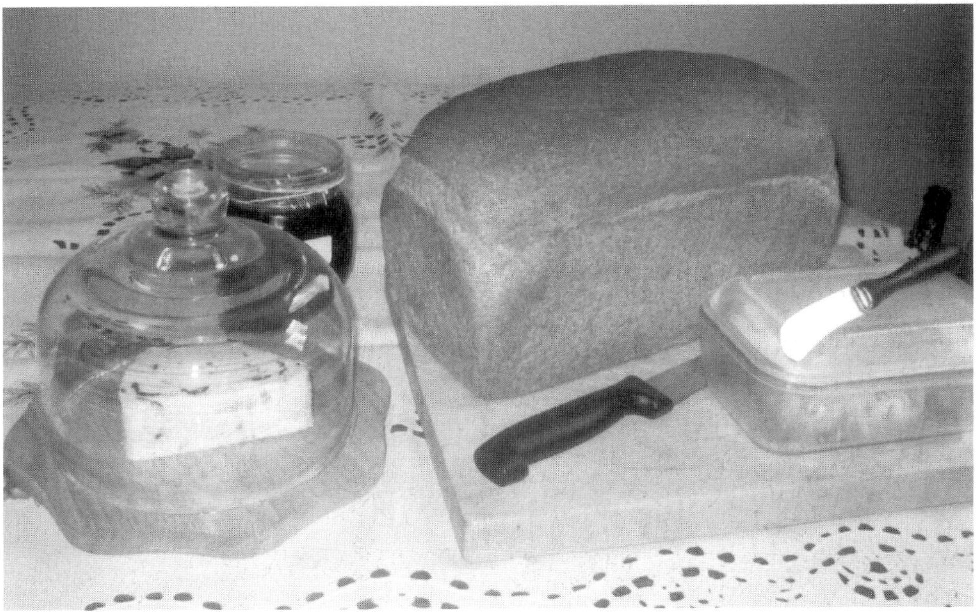

Wholemeal bread. (Photograph courtesy Ron and Barbara Strachan)

General Cornish Recipes

Cornish Pasties

Perhaps the forerunner of the Cornish pasty was known as Cornish 'hoggan', a lump of unleavened dough embedded with pieces of pork. From a number of versions and treading on hallowed ground, here is a standard recipe.

The story that the original pasties, which were eaten in the mines 100 years ago, were sweet at one end and savoury at the other, thus providing two courses for a hungry miner, was taken seriously in Mevagissey by Stephen Grocutt. Known as the 'Big Un' by friends because of his physical stature and his pasties, in his busy shop in July 1988, he ushered in a traditional steak and apple form.

The Job Creation Team at Pendennis Castle which was headed by Bob Timmins, insisted that a pasty was non-genuine without fish at one end and meat at the other, the fish head hanging out to prevent him drinking the gravy! (Were they pulling my leg?) The mention of pasties caused them to render the Oggy Song:

OY, OY, OY, how happy I will be
When I go to the West Countree.

However, we found that fishermen do not take a pasty to sea any more than a Lancashire trawlerman would have on board a woman, a parson or a pork pie.

All the pasties we tried, including those at the King Arthur Café at Tintagel, tasted wonderful after we had been flattened by Atlantic winds whilst walking on the cliffs and exploring caverns.

A true Cornish pasty is a hard act to follow and I am ashamed to say that the Lancashire version is so confused that it uses pre-cooked potatoes and corned beef, although it still manages to smell good.

As we drew into St Ives it seemed there was a pasty in every mouth and the seagulls wanted a taste too.

Jugged Cornish Kippers

This is the simplest meal but perfect for a kipper lover.

Place kippers' heads downwards into a large jug so that they stand upright. Pour boiling water over them. Only the tips of the tails should remain uncovered. Leave for five minutes then drain and pat dry. At this point remove heads and tails. Serve with brown bread and butter.

Practice makes perfect at handling the many bones but the boiling water seems to make it easier.

Courgettes and Tomatoes (A Cornish chef's idea)

Ingredients

6 garlic cloves, peeled and sliced
3 tablespoons of virgin olive oil (virgin olive oil from the first pressing of the olives has the most delicate flavour)
Young courgettes (should not need peeling)
4 sun-dried tomatoes, sliced
Grated cheese

Method

- ❖ Fry the garlic cloves in the olive oil, then discard garlic.
- ❖ Cut the courgettes into chunks, and add to the olive oil with the tomatoes.
- ❖ Sprinkle with the cheese.
- ❖ Put into an ovenproof dish and bake in at 160°C/gas mark 3 for 40 minutes.

Spring Salad (From the same chef)

Ingredients for the salad

12oz (350g) small new potatoes, scrubbed and quartered
½ cucumber
4 ripe tomatoes, cut into quarters
1oz (25g) olives, pitted and halved
3oz (75g) cheese, diced
1 small onion, very thinly sliced
1 tablespoon of freshly chopped mint

Ingredients for the dressing

3 tablespoons of virgin olive oil
1 clove of garlic, crushed
1 tablespoon of cider vinegar
Sea salt and freshly ground black pepper

Method

- ❖ Simmer potatoes for 15 minutes until tender. Drain and cool.
- ❖ Combine with the other salad ingredients.
- ❖ Put the dressing ingredients into a screw-topped jar and shake well.
- ❖ Pour the dressing over the salad.

Cornish Dumplings

Just as Cornish pasties with meat at one end and fruit or jam at the other were carried down tin mines, so were Cornish dumplings taken into the fields by agricultural labourers and consumed for 'bever' or mid-morning snack.

Percy B. Birtchnell said, 'This dumpling depended for its success upon a sound interdepartmental wall', presumably so that the sweet and savoury twain never met. One housewife left a protruding piece of straw or 'plait' to indicate the meat end for her good man. Again, specifics were missing but this intriguing dumpling had to be tried out. Suet, universally once a great filler taking the edge off appetite, figured widely ages past, in every county we visited.

> Make the suet pastry by mixing 4oz grated beef suet, ½lb flour, 3 oz breadcrumbs and binding with a little cold water to form a soft dough. Roll out and cut pastry into individual pieces about 6in sq. Raise a middle 'wall'. Fill on either side using chopped pork or bacon one end, chopped, sugary apple at the other, crimping edges of pastry together.

The dumplings were traditionally boiled in a clean cloth. Even if the two-way system breaks down it still tastes good!

Cornish Wild Strawberry Syllabub

Captain William Stackhouse Pinwill's mansion at Trehare was famous for cream teas with strawberries and peaches grown there in the late nineteenth century. Sadly the great house was burnt down.

The strawberries are small and sweet, less plentiful now, but raspberries can be used instead.

Method

- Whip the cream until it peaks then whip in the brandy and honey.
- Fold in the fruit.
- Divide the syllabub into chilled glasses.

Ingredients

½ pint (275ml) thick Cornish cream

8oz (225g) wild strawberries

2 tablespoons of brandy

1 tablespoon of honey

Glossary

Bever	a mid-morning snack
Christmas lambswool	wassail
Faggots	a bundle of sticks bound together as fuel/a ball of s easoned, chopped liver, baked or fried
Flitch	a side of bacon
Fuggan	pastry
Furze	gorse
Oggy	slang for Cornish pasty
Ookner	part of a range
Pipkin	a small earthenware pot
Range	a large cooking stove with several burners or hotplates

Hints from Cornish Cooks

'Make a friend of a Cornishman and he is a friend for life', we were told in our journeyings. Here are some tips we received from friends when collecting recipes.

Food revolves around the rhythm of the seasons, cooler, wetter summers have meant demand for hot food all year round.

Beans, lentils and chick peas should be soaked well and cooked well. Leave out salt as it retards softening.

Cornish 'eggyot' is good for preventing colds. Beat 2 eggs with 1 teaspoon of sugar. Pour a quart (2 pints) of hot cider on this and drink whilst hot.

Small savoury dumplings can be made by pounding pigs' liver with breadcrumbs and herbs, binding with a little egg yolk. They are useful for dropping in stews about ½ hour before dishing up.

Clean fig leaves can be used to wrap small portions of meat, dates, etc to give flavour in cooking.

Aubergines should be soaked for one hour in salted water and gently squeezed before use.

Unglazed earthenware cooking utensils over charcoal fires result in the best flavours.

'The good cook tastes as he goes. Not only is it his privilege, it is necessary to get the flavours right'.

To rescue over-salted dishes, add a few spoonfuls of milk or put a pound of raw potato in the middle of the dish. A lump of sugar left in for a few minutes also helps.

Soak cabbage, spinach, etc in ½lb salt dissolved in water. Rinse well with cold water after 20 minutes. This kills insects which will sink to the bottom.

A cloth, well steeped in vinegar, placed over the pan, lessens the strong smell when cooking vegetables. Alternatively, add 2 bay leaves to the water.

Never add bicarbonate of soda to the water when cooking greens. Plunge the greens in fast-boiling water for no more than 10 minutes.

Olives will keep better when the jar is opened if you add a dessertspoon of oil to the brine.

Iced water helps to crisp a lettuce.

One dessertspoon of flour added to the water helps to keep cauliflower white.

Cooked potatoes intended for salad will absorb less oil and taste better if they are sprinkled with white wine whilst still warm after the boiling.

Crab or lobster should feel heavy, look fresh and have no cracks in their shells.

Traditionally the best way is to boil. 'Leave thermidors, mousses and bisques to the bogles'.

Tomatoes can easily be skinned by pouring boiling water over them; oranges are more easily peeled this way, pith comes away with peel. Unless apples are home grown, a scalding is necessary to remove the wax coating.

Shell boiled eggs under running water.

Beat air into cake mixtures with the flat of the hand. Under the mixing bowl, when using it tilted, place a thick, folded damp cloth to prevent skidding.

In bread making, a crushed Vitamin C tablet added with the sugar gets a better result. Clotted cream is traditionally made from fresh cow's milk; pasteurised will not do. It was placed in large, shallow pans on a shelf of the 'slab' on low heat. The cream rises and the heavy crust is skimmed off.

Grow and use your own herbs, there is no substitute for them. Most flourish in Cornwall. Sprigs of herbs make attractive garnishings. Chives, parsley and tarragon do not dry well, but those that do, bay leaves, thyme and lemon balm are roughly three times more concentrated.

The secret of cooking venison is to marinate it first and lard well during cooking.

Young grouse should be roasted, stuffed with moorland raspberries or served with home-made rowan jelly. Older ones need to be marinated in casseroles.

Old rabbits need marinating; young can be roasted with a coating of mustard or stewed in cider.

Old hares need to be marinated in red wine for at least 24 hours and slow cooked. Leverets or young hares roast well accompanied with redcurrant jelly. Potted hare and hare pie was once traditional.

Young partridges should be roasted, served with watercress and breadcrumbs or accompaniments. The carcase makes a rich soup.

The last word: 'Cornish pasties are perfect with a mug of West Country cider'.

Other titles published by The History Press

Cornish Pioneers and the Odd Villain

BOB RICHARDS

Celebrating gallant individuals like John Goyne, the Gold Rush pioneer, *Cornish Pioneer and the Odd Villain* provides an insight into the lives of some of the Cornish men and women who have helped shape the history of the county. Cornwall has produced its fai share of celebrated sons and daughters, but it has also produced some unlikely heroes, pioneers and the odd villain. The book will not only appeal to all those who are interes in Cornwall and its people, but also to anyone who simply likes a good adventure story.

978 0 7524 4713 1

Cornwall Strange But True

JOAN RENDELL

Well-known local author Joan Rendell presents a guide to over 100 of the strangest and most remarkable sights in Cornwall. This entertaining book describes curious and unusual buildings, objects and landscape features that have survived the centuries. It is aims to inspire many to explore the highways and byways of Cornwall, and is ideal for those who love to roam the countryside.

978 0 7509 4623 0

Haunted Cornwall

PAUL NEWMAN

For anyone who would like to know why Cornwall is called the most haunted place i Britain, this collection of stories of apparitions, manifestations and related supernatural incidents provides the answer. From heart-stopping accounts of poltergeists to first-hand encounters with ghouls and spirits who haunt prehistoric graves, *Haunted Cornw* contains a chilling range of ghostly phenomena.

978 0 7524 3668 5

Herring: A History of the Silver Darlings

MIKE SMYLIE

The story of herring is entwined in the history of commercial fishing. For over two millennia, herring has been commercially caught and its importance to the coastal peo of Britain cannot be measured. At one point tens of thousands were involved in the catching, processing and sale of herring. Many towns on the East Coast grew rich on t backs of the silver darlings. In addition, for those who have neglected the silver darling for lesser fish such as cod or haddock, there are numerous recipes to try!

978 0 7524 2988 5